FREEDOM TO LEARN

CHOOSING YOUR PATH TO HOMESCHOOLING VICTORY

LEILANI MELENDEZ

Freedom to Learn:
Choosing Your Path to Homeschooling Victory
© 2022 by Leilani Melendez

Printed in the United States of America

ISBN-13: 979-8-9865252-0-4

DEDICATION

I am dedicating this book to all the parents out there who may feel stuck, frustrated, exhausted, or who may just need a little encouragement or redirection to keep going. It's my hope that you find it to be a breath of fresh air as God guides you and your family on your homeschool journey.

INTRODUCTION

*M*ost people think it's just a natural progression of life. Raising kids is just what you do when you're in your twenties, thirties, and forties. But I see this as a calling. The reality is, though, that not everyone has this opportunity. This opportunity is actually the highest of all opportunities. We are entrusted to raise little humans in a chaotic world, decide what we think is best for them, and then guide them as they make life decisions. They rely on us more than we'll ever know. We are their world, their mentor, their best friend. Every decision they make is indirectly influenced by us. Our impact on their lives is incomparable to any other job... and it's the best job, ever!

Every parent has the right to make the best decision for their kids. This includes education, too. In a world where education has been programmed and schooling has been designed for the masses, parents can be pressured—even brainwashed—into doing what they truly do not want to do. Even within the homeschool movement, parents feel obligated to teach against the nature of who their child is, feel as though they have to meet certain goals, use a certain curriculum, and form their child into a human being that they themselves have been pressured into molding. In the end, they feel unsatisfied, frustrated, and alone.

As a Homeschool Evaluator, former teacher, and mom, I see this all the time. Parents are worried and they need reassurance. Reassurance that they are not crazy for thinking that what they want is what is best. They need a reassuring voice with first-hand experience to bring that to them. This is where I step in.

I have met with many families over the years. During our evaluation and testing sessions, we look through their child's work and talk about their progression. We even discuss their goals and passions. I answer questions about how homeschooling usually works, and I even give my best advice. I can honestly, and humbly, say that after I walk out of their homes, many parents feel empowered. They realize that they always knew what was best, and now they can begin to step into that.

I am also very passionate about working with parents of kids who have special needs. This can be a whole different, and even isolating, world. I love reaching out to these families and letting them know that they are not alone, that they are not failing their child, that they are still in control, and honestly, that what they are experiencing emotionally is normal. As my youngest daughter has Downs Syndrome, I understand all of this, not only from an educator's perspective, but as a mom.

In addition to all of this, I have a YouTube channel where I influence thousands of viewers a month—not just homeschool parents, but also parents of kids who have special needs and learning disabilities. My channel offers parents hope by showing them that they are not alone in this journey. With all of my experience as a professional teacher and all my training as an educator, I still find myself learning.

But I also find that, through my experiences, I am able to share helpful tips and advice that the struggling homeschool parents can use to thrive and succeed. I want to see every parent empowered to do exactly what they were created to do.

On my channel, I've made videos that range from different homeschool philosophies to homeschooling laws. I've shared my struggles with getting my kids to finish their work, how we considered vacation as learning, and I even share ideas to help parents of kids with special needs navigate through this homeschool world. My videos have reached thousands of viewers worldwide, and I have no idea how many people I have influenced. I'll never meet them or see them face to face, but I am still thankful that I have made an impact on their lives.

Before I was a homeschool mom, I was a professional teacher in both private and public schools. Students would grace me with their presence every year, and I am thankful for all that they've taught me regarding their independence and uniqueness.

Unfortunately, I also saw first-hand how these students were treated as just another name and number, how decisions were made based on rules and regulations rather than who they were or how they learned. I watched as students with special needs were brushed aside and hidden in a classroom away from everyone else to be merely babysat by a substitute teacher because no one could be found to fill the position. Around test time, I saw the anxiety level increase for everyone. I saw students rise in popularity based on their success, while other students are trampled on based on their failures.

Worst of all, I witnessed the lies and deceit that were fed to students through bad procedures and curricula to brainwash them to be something they were not, fashioning them instead into what "the system" wanted them to be.

The trust that we have lost over the years from our schools, politicians, public school curriculum writers, and teachers has only increased. It forces us to seek a better alternative, yet they still hold us in bondage.

Ultimately, I feel a tremendous burden to see families break free and be who they are meant to be.

My hope for this book is that it reaches the parent who is struggling to rediscover their purpose, the parent so burnt out that all they want to do is give up even though they know it would be going against their calling. I hope this book reaches that parent who worries, thinking they have ruined their child's future, the parent who is afraid to find out what the future holds for them, the parent who feels like they have failed. I hope this book reaches the homeschool parent who feels alone, isolated, frustrated, scared, and hopeless.

In this book, you will find wisdom and truth, and you will find encouragement and motivation to just keep going. Nothing in this world need hold you back from being that parent you were meant to be, and nothing should hold your child back, either.

It's never too late to break free, and that is what you will get from this book—a renewed sense of freedom.

You were created to homeschool your child. If you weren't, you wouldn't be reading this book. But you feel it deep down inside your soul: these are your children, your family; no one else on this planet can replace them. No one else on this planet understands them more than you. I understand this feeling, because I, too, feel this deeply.

I pray that as you read this book the chains will be loosened. Your eyes will be opened. You will find yourself laughing, playing, and holding your children as you learn together, no matter what age they are. You are their teacher, their parent, and their mentor.

Special Consideration

As a Believer in Messiah, much of my ideas and thoughts are inspired by biblical teachings; it is the foundation of how I think. However, I know not everyone thinks this way.

So, when I wrote this book, I wanted everyone to glean from it, regardless of faith or belief. But, I didn't want to deny the Creator of all of this. He is the essence of life itself and everything that makes me who I am.

So, I did two things. First, I randomly included acknowledgement of Him when it was necessary through the book without going on a tangent. It is nothing that will offend anyone. In fact, you may not even notice that it's there.

Second, I included points where I take a "Spiritual Moment." Here, I sum up the chapter or section with God at the forefront. It is meant to put everything into perspective within a Christian worldview. It is my heart and soul.

If you choose to skip these sections, I understand. But for those of us that need this encouragement, including me, it is there. It is there for us so we can take time to lean on Him, and recognize His handiwork and providence over all of our lives. Without the Lord, this book would not be possible, so I have no choice but to take time to glorify Him.

Either way, I hope that you will be immensely blessed by this book, so much so that it changes your life for the better.

TABLE OF CONTENTS

CHAPTER I

THE FEAR OF FREEDOM

Everyone Wants the Best

The moment a mother and father first lay eyes on their precious child, we decide then and there that we want what's best for them. We want the best doctors to care for them. We want the best home for them that will provide stability and peace. We want our kids to have the nicest friends and neighborhood playmates. We even want our children to have the best education and every opportunity to succeed in their future careers. We are determined—and we promised ourselves that nothing was going to stop us.

Most of us live in a country filled with choices. These are freedoms that some people can only dream of having. We can choose our career path, our partner, the food we eat, and much more. We can even choose how our children are educated. The choices seem almost limitless. Why would we not choose the best path for our children?

And some of us chose to homeschool. Why not? There are so many reasons why many parents decided to go down this path. It could simply be that they want to reinforce their family values. But the reasons could also range from curriculum issues to teacher and administration concerns. There could be bullying confrontations and even a lack of supervision that could eventually lead to bad influences. Maybe they are concerned that their child is not receiving quality instruction or that the teachers are not equipped to handle their child's special needs situation.

Regardless of the reason, they chose homeschooling. This is their child's childhood. Why not make it the best it could possibly be?

Why Do We Limit Ourselves?

Homeschooling is a dedicated option that many parents choose to take. We have the best reasons in the world to do it. We are motivated, encouraged, and obsessed. We write down our goals and purposes, and swear that nothing is going to stop us. But sometimes we get stuck, overwhelmed, and frustrated. We actually limit ourselves. We forget why we started homeschooling in the first place and we want to give up.

The decisions were so easy when we were just holding our child in our arms, but then they grew up. They developed personalities, strengths, and weaknesses. At the same time, we now had the weight of the world on our shoulders. The joy of homeschooling disappears and we have no idea where it went. The dreams we had for our newborn baby are forgotten, and we fall in lockstep with so many others.

What Really Goes On

As a homeschooling mom of four, a homeschool evaluator, and a former school teacher who taught in both public and private schools, I have worked with many families and have seen many different personalities, and even disabilities. I see the same pattern over and over—a pattern that brings parents down and makes them feel uncertain about their child's future if they should continue to walk through this journey.

Too many parents suffer through each day, pushing through just to get to the evening so they can have their cup of coffee (or wine) in peace. They scroll through their social media feeds only to feel less and less like a person and more and more like the scum on the bottom of a barrel. The blessing of being a parent no longer feels like a gift but a burden or a curse.

You dwell on how you've wasted away your day, yelling at your kids, scoffing at their school assignment, then wondering if you've done enough. You see other parents smiling in their Instagram photos, sharing their latest trip to the zoo, museum, or park. Then you look at your life and you think that your success lies in the fact that they got out of their pajamas. Is this what you sacrificed for?

You chose not to do public school. Instead, you choose to work with your child in a positive environment. But it turned out to be anything but that. You constantly keep wondering if your child has fallen behind. If so, how far? In what areas? You wonder if your curriculum is missing the mark if there are any educational holes. Should you have them tested? If so, what standardized test should you use? Is it possible to even redeem the time you wasted on the wrong teaching styles or curricula? Did you make a mistake? Have you ruined your child? Did you set them up for failure? Your head is full of questions and concerns, and the more you wonder, the more you realize that the clock is ticking.

By nature, homeschooling goes against the grain.

It is an uncomfortable reality. You are outside the norm. Your family is outside the norm. You are already unique and everyone has questions. But they also have opinions, and they are not always so quick to refrain from speaking. You will get hurt. And as you receive the criticism from family, friends, coworkers, or acquaintances, you start to wonder if homeschooling is worth it. You might continue homeschooling, but slowly incorporate what society tells you to teach. Where are the benchmarks to tell you what your child needs?

You stop listening to your child and start listening to others. As much as your kids fight back, you keep pushing. They scream, "This is not me," but you yell back, "This is what you are supposed to be." Eventually, you forget why you chose to homeschool in the first place. And eventually, your home looks nothing like what you've dreamed. Your relationship with your child is slowly breaking. Homeschooling no longer brings joy and you wonder if it is the best thing for your child.

But there is hope.

It's time to open your eyes to the wonderful freedoms that homeschooling allows. You don't have to be like anyone else in order to be successful. God made each of us unique, crafted for a unique purpose. Instead of trying to mold your children to whatever trend is happening or to whatever your friend told you to do, or even to the benchmarks, learn to discover what your child needs.

If this is what you need, then it's time to change your mindset and think outside the box, beyond educational standards and rigorous demands.

You are the parent, and you have the right to choose how your child will be educated. Just realizing this will bring you the peace you need to continue on this journey. You will be able to think outside the box and meet the needs of your child, however that may look. The fear of not measuring up will no longer matter. There is no need for "measuring up."

No one compares to you, your family, and your family's culture and beliefs. There is no fear of missing out. You will see that in everything, in every little thing, God has provided.

If you want to change the climate of your home, if you need encouragement, if you want your eyes opened to what homeschooling should be, then this is the book for you. Understanding the freedoms you have as a homeschool family will not only bring you peace, but will also allow your relationship with your kids to flourish. If you're ready for this adventure then it's time to open your eyes to the reality of raising children. Yes, there will be bumps along the way, but they won't bother you if you truly change your perspective.

CHAPTER II

WHY?

Why do you homeschool?

*D*o you remember the moment you decided to homeschool? Do you remember what it was that made you decide? Was it by choice or out of necessity? Did you feel relieved to be in charge, or did you feel fearful and overwhelmed?

What happened when you started? Was it an immediate success, or did everything just crash down on you? Maybe you didn't know where to start or who to trust. Regardless, now you feel stuck and are seeking out direction. You are motivated. That is why you are here.

Why did I decide to homeschool?

For me, like most every parent, I love my children. As a teacher, I was around many children all day long, but none of them were as special to me as mine.

At the age of 31, I decided to homeschool. I had confidence in my teaching ability; I knew I could pull this off. I was also frustrated with what the public schools had to offer me as a parent. I knew it just wasn't part of what I wanted for my family. I knew that I wanted a different environment for my children.

The day I made my official decision was when I was walking to the school office to file some paperwork during my lunch break. My second son kicked my stomach again making lunch a fleeting thought. On my way, a student of mine was wandering the halls. He had autism, and the special needs substitute teacher had given him a hall pass so that he could go visit his mother who was also a teacher. He clearly was not going in that direction. Since I had a good relationship with him, I felt comfortable asking him more about his wandering goals.

Eventually, I was able to guide him to the proper place. But this was not the first this had happened, nor would it be the last time. I was fully aware of this, and I was also aware that my school was not the only school with lack of supervision. I was concerned.

After my detour that day, as I continued on my journey to the office, God spoke very clearly.

I was to homeschool.

And for the first time, I felt peace about my children's future childhood. I felt peace about resigning from my job and trusting that God would provide for our family. It was my first step on this homeschooling journey, which I would later discover, was truly a journey.

Six months later, with the encouragement of my husband (whose initial response to my desire to homeschool was, "It's about time!"), I resigned from teaching public school. I had a newborn boy and a two-year-old son, my husband had a fairly new job, and we just downsized to a new home. We were hopeful, we felt encouraged, and I was ready to take on the new adventure.

I would be lying if I told you it was easy. It wasn't. Money was tight. And honestly, I missed my job. My heart was divided. To get my fix, I took on a part-time position as a private school teacher for low-income students that needed extra support. I also shared my talents with a local homeschool co-op as a science teacher.

8

As my boys grew, I became more and more engrossed in the homeschool movement. As I learned more, my desire to help encourage parents increased. I learned that every family is unique, and it's that uniqueness that makes our world so distinct.

I learned about the homeschool laws in our state (Florida) and started evaluating and testing homeschool students in order to help them meet their legal requirements. I learned that every parent is qualified and capable of teaching their kids.

I also learned that so many parents feel helpless and fearful, and they worry that they are not doing enough.

There is so much more I learned through this experience, and am still learning, to be honest. It's never ending. However, there is one valuable lesson that trumps all others.

The Parent is in Control

Yes, that is so true. You, their parent, have the right to be in control of your child's learning. That is the most valuable lesson I learned.

And that could look like anything. Do you believe this? Is this something you can take ownership of? Does it make sense?

Do you understand that God chose you to raise these kids? That, if you have the desire in your heart, no matter the circumstance, you are capable. You are qualified.

There is a reason you chose to homeschool. It could be any reason in the world. But sometimes, we cannot pinpoint the exact reason.

We are going to look at that. In addition, we are going to look at the importance of goal-setting. Do you have homeschooling goals? What drives you? What keeps you going? Having a plan is essential for moving forward. A plan gives you purpose, motivation, and focus.

We are also going to look at when and why public schooling began. The public school system we know of today is actually fairly new. Before this, it was common for kids to have private tutors, be sent off to special schools, or were simply schooled at home. Many children just enjoyed learning. They explored their passions and they became who they needed to be because they had the freedom to be who they were meant to be.

As homeschool parents, we have the freedom to provide that opportunity for our own children. It takes some planning, and it takes some prayer. But with the right mindset, understanding of the truth, and motivation, you will be able to succeed, with joy, through this homeschool journey.

You will be renewed. You will be encouraged. You will be empowered.

Change is Inevitable

When my fourth child was born, I took one look at her and realized our parenting journey was about to change. We had three beautiful kids, all with unique personalities. In my mind, their early childhood was already mapped out. I had near-future plans for them; I even had a curriculum planned for them. But even simple things like which rooms they would sleep in, where the majority of our money and time would go, all of this was planned. But the plan needed to change. I needed to become flexible.

My fourth child was born with a heart defect and also had Down Syndrome. She would require therapies for probably the majority of her life and intensely through her childhood. Invasive heart surgery was needed within the first year of her life in order for her to live. Until she was ready, she would require under careful watch and needed weekly doctor visits to make sure she was thriving and growing.

Everything that I had dreamed of was basically thrown out the window. It sucked! It sucked for the first few months, but let me reassure you, these dreams were eventually replaced with new dreams and the old curriculum was replaced with what was needed for our family at that time. Instead of allowing myself to be bound to the norm, to what I thought was expected of me, I had no choice but to embrace the freedom I had.

As homeschoolers, we have that freedom, the freedom to adjust to what our family needs in every given moment of our lives. We are not in bondage to the norms of society, or to what the public schools deem important. We don't need to adjust to them when a curveball or bump in the road occurs. Instead of focusing on that, focus on what matters most: we are accountable to God and to our family. If you can remember that, homeschooling will be a lot more enjoyable.

But it's not always that easy. Saying it is much easier than doing it. So, let me give you some tools and thoughts that can help you begin to change your understanding and presuppositions. With knowledge comes confidence, and with confidence you will know that you are capable.

CHAPTER III

TRAGEDY

I was alone with my sons in the back room again. This was pretty normal now. You see, every Saturday we attended services, and every Saturday the boys felt the need to just be loud. What else would one expect from a three- and a four-year-old?

But today was different. Today, I had to share a room with another gentleman, one who was well respected in the community. Whatever reason he had for being here in the back room, I had no idea.

The gentleman was very kind and appropriate. My boys just thought he was fun. I had known him and his family for years, and quite frankly, it was pleasant company. We casually chatted, at first, but I don't know where the conversation went or why he felt the need to insult me and my choice to eventually homeschool, but he did. It had to do with the social and emotional well-being of my son. The words were as sharp as a knife and they cut to the bone. It was a personal statement directed toward my parenting skills and the flaws he already saw in my son.

Even worse, he decided that those would be the words he would leave me with. He exited the room without even an attempt to listen to a rebuttal. Which was just as well as I couldn't speak. Tears and self-doubt clouded my

13

vision. I sat there alone, contemplating my next thought. What seemed like hours were actually only seconds.

A sweet friend broke the silence as she entered the room. She was only seventeen, but I trusted her. In fact she had babysat my boys a few times.

"What's wrong?" she asked.

She looked at me with concern as I began telling her what had just happened. The details of the conversation poured out, and with every word self-doubt poured in. Then I repeated the words he spoke, how they hit like daggers, and how he left abruptly.

Her face never changed, but her eyes drew me in.

"How well do you know his kids?" she began. "Have you seen how they turned out?

And how many wives has he had? Sure, he's respected for what he does outside of his home, but look at the fruit of his family. His kids don't even want to be around him. Does he have room to speak these words into your life? Especially when it comes to parenting."

This seventeen-year-old girl continued to speak as if she had the seasoned wisdom of a fifty-year-old mother.

"You are an amazing mother. You love your kids and provide for everything they need. No one in the world will care for them like you do. Sure, they will stumble, and sure, you will run into obstacles, but I know you. You will figure out how to overcome them together as a family unit."

You might be asking, how on earth did she gain so much wisdom at such a young age?

Well, for one, she was homeschooled in a household of five other siblings.

I'll tell you what has become of her later in the book. But first, let me take you back to when her parents decided to homeschool. Let me share with you the true story of a family that made strong choices and defied everyone's expectations despite the situations that fell upon them.

Angela's Story

Her mom, like most moms, never considered homeschooling until they met a homeschooling family and talked with a homeschooling mom. Angela was very impressed with this woman. She had nine children, and the oldest one had just received an academic scholarship from Yale to play football. So, that in and of itself, was impressive.

Nine years later, Angela's family had grown. Her older kids were attending public school, and all was not going as planned. The oldest boy was a struggling reader and was behind in many classes. To add to that, her husband did not like how the school taught handwriting. Such a simple thing, but for him it was a big deal.

The couple prayed hard and discussed their options. Finally, in March of 2004, they decided to withdraw their children from public school. And by May of 2004, both kids had caught up to the first grade "state standards" in reading.

The question Angela faced now was...

"Do I send them back to school, or continue on this homeschooling journey?"

Angela decided to attend conferences. She browsed at a local store that had a lot of homeschool resources. By the fall, she felt confident to continue on the homeschool path.

Along with the curriculum she picked out, she got her kids involved with Cub Scouts and American Heritage Girls. They went on campouts and got involved with local service projects. They also got involved with an accelerated learning program for math as well as the YMCA for "homeschooling" PE.

For two years, Angela succeeded at providing all of the curriculum and extra activities that were needed to give her kids a well-rounded education. Not to mention that her husband was moving up career-wise in the world and they were planning a big move.

Everything was looking really good for them.

Then she received a phone call.

While her husband was out running a few business errands to tie up some loose ends before the move, a car rammed his vehicle. It killed him.

No woman can even imagine how devastating a tragic car accident can be until your provider, your best friend, and partner is killed. There are no words to even describe what she felt. She was now a young mother of six young kids, widowed. In fact, her youngest was only a few months old.

How was she going to provide? How was she going to coach them through healing when she needed time to heal herself? Was homeschool even an option anymore?

Several of her friends suggested that she put the older three in public school to allow her time to heal. And that seemed like good, well-meaning advice. But she also knew that her children were broken, too. They needed their mother. So, instead of throwing them out, she drew them in. They cried together, comforted each other, and prayed together.

Then, they continued on with co-ops and activities as though life was normal.

As a mother with wisdom, she knew that too much change too fast would be too much. She was sensitive to their needs and met them where they were at, assuring them that not only she was there, but most importantly, God was.

Of course, life happens, and they had to make some changes. They were forced out of their home and had to put all of their belongings in storage.

Over the four months that followed, they prayed and petitioned the Lord and He provided them with housing.

She said, "The first family we stayed with helped watch my kids while I moved our things into storage with hired help. The family had a guest room and a playroom where the older two could sleep on air mattresses. Next, we were able to find a family that needed a house-sitter. We house-sat while they were away for a few weeks. After that, another friend allowed us to stay for five weeks while her husband was away on a business trip."

This was their life for a while.

The lawsuit was finalized, they received a settlement, and were then able to have some closure.

The next plan was to purchase an RV and head eastward.

The cabinets were shoved full with homeschool supplies, minimal kitchen utensils, and enough clothes to keep them warm and dry. To help with the move, they adopted two little dogs that attached themselves to the kids quickly.

The journey wasn't an easy one. They first tried to visit with family in Atlanta and various cities in North Carolina, hoping that someone would help them to feel welcome. They also wanted to find the right congregation.

"For several months, we would go to an area to visit, spend some time with family, some time on school work, and then look around to see if that area was a good fit."

Eventually they found their home in Charlotte, North Carolina where they found an amazing congregation that welcomed them with open arms. There was also a great Boy Scouts organization and homeschool community.

With a transformational life change like this, one does not continue homeschooling the same way. Angela's philosophies changed. Her focus was now on what mattered in life: her God and her family. She learned to relax the schedule when needed and flow with each child as they approached each day. She didn't get hung up on the little things in life anymore. There was no need. Life was too short.

More and more each day, she learned to put God first. She made it a point to teach her children values, compassion, discernment, and wisdom. This way, they could survive and thrive in this world.

She considered her new philosophy "relaxed homeschooling," but really it didn't matter what they called it. They were doing life, learning, trusting, and growing. Even though it was a nontraditional form of schooling, come test time, all of her kids were doing well.

Thankfully, every person is unique...

Every family is unique and every situation is unique. When you decide to homeschool, you are embracing that individuality and building roots within your home that will always bring you and your family back to what you value. No one has your path, your experiences, your mindset, and your culture. You are unique.

What you do at your home would have never worked for Angela's situation—or vice-versa. She had to adapt and mold into what was needed for them to thrive. Going the "normal" route or the public-school route would have separated them from what they loved most. But, even if she had stuck with traditional homeschooling, arguments might have erupted frequently, priorities would have been shelved, the healing they needed might have never occurred.

But, that is not the only lesson to learn from this story. With determination and perseverance, if homeschooling is what you've been called to do, nothing can stop you.

You might also ask how her kids turned out. Were they socially awkward? Were they "Momma's boys?" Did they even go to college?

I think it's extremely important to see the outcome of the children in everyone's stories. It gives you hope, encouragement, and motivation to know that when you put their needs first (as opposed to yours or the community's), you really can't mess things up.

Angela's first son went on to be a mechanic after finishing school. He is a husband, a hard worker, a sustainer, and a father. The second, ironically, became a public school teacher. This was after she pursued her own business and hobby as a comic book artist. She still does that on the side, but teaching is her full-time job.

The third daughter is the girl I spoke about at the beginning of the chapter. She is a cosmetologist and works in a salon. However, she is currently taking a break from that career as she pursues the hardest job of them all, motherhood. She also does a lot of volunteer work on the side to help out her community for fun.

The fourth daughter is currently working on her college degree in architecture and drafting.

The two youngest are still in high school as I write this. They are still figuring out life and what lies ahead for them.

After speaking many times to Angela, she has regrets, too. But it's not, "I didn't push them enough," or, "I wish I'd started algebra earlier."

"In looking back," Angela says, "I would have only chosen to stay in the RV and traveled longer. It would have been great to spend time seeing the country together, using even that opportunity as a path to learn more about our country."

Learning about our country or the country you live in is so important. Before we really can understand why we do things the way we do or why we live with certain standards, we must know the history behind things. Have you ever wondered about the history of education and the philosophies behind it? The next chapter will help you get started on that journey.

CHAPTER IV

A Super-Brief History
of Education

I HAVE NEVER LET SCHOOLING INTERFERE WITH MY EDUCATION.
MARK TWAIN

Everyone is Being Educated

Schooling and Educating are two slightly different things. Everyone receives some kind of education—period. You can be educated in cooking, engineering, auto mechanics, pet care, or even driving. You can be educated on the streets of New York or at Yale.

Now schooling is a place that provides a specific kind of education. Schooling can happen at home, in the formal public-school environment, or at a specialty academy such as police, fire, or theatre academy.

Since the beginning of time and since the first person set foot on this earth, there has been some sort of educating going on. Formal schooling has also been a popular option, but schooling has looked very different through the ages, and some schools were limited to specific types of people.

In ancient Egypt, the rich, and the children of physicians and temple administrators were among the few that were schooled; the rest of the children schooled with their parents. Boys learned a trade from their father, and girls focused on motherhood, housekeeping, and cooking.

In ancient Israel, nothing mattered more to the people than the Torah. The High Priest opened special schools called Yeshivas to help students focus specifically on reading, memorizing, oral repetition, teaching and writing of the Torah. In Islamic civilizations, boys could go to school for free to learn to read, write, and explore the universe. During the Vedic Period of India (1500 to 600 BCE), free schools focused on orally teaching the skills of grammar, composition, nature, logic, science, and the skills needed for an occupation to name just a few. Women were taught music, dance, and housekeeping.

In Greece, private schools were the way to go. The only exception was Sparta, where the schools were focused on creating warriors with complete obedience, courage, and physical perfection. But Greece was very unique in that anyone could open up a school on whatever they wanted to teach. There were schools on music, writing, and even gymnastics and sports. Parents could send their boys to whatever school they wanted and for however long they wanted. Even poorer families could send their children to school for a few years for a reasonable fee.

In the Middle Ages, the Roman Catholic Church dominated the schools, which came to be known as Christian monastic schools. These schools, called scriptorias, focused specifically on book copying. Even though the kings and churches took education seriously, only a few were educated in these schools.

When it comes to the history of schooling and education, this is only the tip of the tip of the iceberg, but still you can see a pattern. Religion and faith played a major role in how children were being educated. So did one's place in society, one's status, one's family, and one's gender. Not everyone was educated in a school. The majority of kids were educated at home, and that was considered normal.

Suzannah Knew

Suzannah was a brilliant Christian mother—hard-working, and dedicated to her family. She had no choice but to find work in order to raise her seven children. After her husband died at the age of thirty-nine, she single-handedly opened her own grocery store. People adored her, and as a result, it became one of the most successful stores in the little Township in Philadelphia County.

What she wasn't always aware of was the adoring eyes of her son, Benjamin. She adored him as well, and knew that he had a special talent. Because of the financial success of her store, she was able to send Benjamin to a school in Maryland at the age of eight, and eventually to the College of New Jersey (which later became known as Princeton). Suzannah knew schooling was not always necessary to be successful in life, but in the mid-1700s, this was the perfect opportunity for Benjamin. He needed this. Like most moms, Suzannah knew and did what was best for her child.

Benjamin loved schooling and was very successful. He amazed everyone by becoming the youngest graduate of the school at the age of fifteen. At this time, Benjamin decided to return home to be with his family and pursue the study of medicine. This was not only a gift he had, but a love.

Medicine was not only his passion, though. His faith and belief in God was, too. Benjamin also believed in his heart that God gave each and every individual, regardless of their race, their gender, or whether they were slave or free, a set of natural rights. If anyone went against these rights, or even denied any of these rights to any individual, they were actually going against the will of God.

His faith was the center of everything that he believed in. It drove his decisions, how he handled situations, and more. From medically debunking the institution of slavery with a pamphlet to signing the well-known Declaration of Independence, his influence stretched across the colonies. His influence was great.

Now his passion for equality and social change provoked him to push for free public schooling. He loved education; it had changed his life.

"A republican nation can never long be free and happy without their citizens being educated," he said. Education was a right that everyone deserved to have. The only way this would be possible would be to provide an equal opportunity to everyone, regardless of their race, gender, or status. Free public education and schooling was his answer.

He was not the only one who believed and pushed for this in the early years of our nation. The Puritans, and many of the founding fathers, even though they may have been homeschooled, supported free public education and schooling for all. But there was a huge difference between what they wanted it to look like then and what it looks like now.

For one, literacy was very important, as, when one is literate, they can read scriptures and vote.

"IN A REPUBLIC WHERE ALL VOTES FOR PUBLIC OFFICERS ARE GIVEN BY BALLOT, SHOULD NOT A KNOWLEDGE OF READING AND WRITING BE CONSIDERED AS ESSENTIAL QUALIFICATIONS FOR AN ELECTOR?"

BENJAMIN RUSH

Religion was also important.

"...THE ONLY FOUNDATION FOR A USEFUL EDUCATION IN A REPUBLIC IS TO BE LAID IN RELIGION. WITHOUT THIS THERE CAN BE NO VIRTUE, AND WITHOUT VIRTUE THERE CAN BE NO LIBERTY, AND LIBERTY IS THE OBJECT AND LIFE OF ALL REPUB-LICAN GOVERNMENTS.... BUT THE RELIGION I MEAN TO RECOM-MEND IS THIS PLACE, IS THAT OF THE NEW TESTAMENT."

BENJAMIN RUSH

When reading his document entitled "Thoughts Upon the Mode of Education Proper in a Republic," one can easily see his vision for free public school. Religion and the study of the New Testament was huge in his mind. In fact, the Bible was pushed as a mandatory textbook.

Public schooling and the motivation for public schooling was very different during the foundation of the United States of America. In fact, it was a completely different model and philosophy than what we have now.

Equality

The idea of equality for all is a very powerful one. The truth of this statement cannot be argued. This philosophy of equality echoes throughout American history, through the Civil War, the Industrial Revolution, and even the World Wars.

Now, in my opinion, Benjamin was just one voice (among many others) that changed the face of education by provoking thoughts and ideas. We will explore the evolution of this idea in the next chapter.

CHAPTER V

THE EVOLUTION OF PUBLIC SCHOOL

"EDUCATION DOES NOT MEAN TEACHING PEOPLE WHAT THEY DO NOT KNOW. IT MEANS TEACHING THEM TO BEHAVE AS THEY DO NOT BEHAVE."

JOHN RUSKIN

The idea of free public schools was a concept that was tossed around for many years, but the purpose was to simply give a free gift—the gift of knowledge. Many saw it as a way to help people read the Bible and understand it on their own, something that European nations had failed to do in the past. Literacy also meant that people could read the voting ballots and vote.

But in walked Horace Mann.

This is when schooling shifted.

Horace Mann was a well-trained, well-educated, and determined politician who was obsessed with making educating free and universal. He spent many days studying different philosophies of education from all over the world, consumed with the thought of finding the best one so that his country could continue to thrive. With his authority and persuasion, when he found one that he liked, he set out to reform education. He even became known as "The Father of American Public School Education."

Meanwhile, over in Europe, Prussia was determined to pick up the pieces and restore pride and greatness within their country and people. One way they sought to do this was through education. After the Napoleonic Wars, Frederick the Great enhanced the education system they had in Prussia— and a lot of countries took notice.

This Prussian method and philosophy of education became known as the Prussian Model.

Let's stop right here, because what you're about to learn is that this is the system that Horace Mann brought to the USA. Canada was similarly inspired by the Prussian Model, as were many other countries.

Given the tremendous influence of the Prussian Model on education around the world, it's important to understand the philosophies behind this method of education. So, let's take a look.

Prussian Education Philosophies

Johann Fichte was an early Prussian philosopher who greatly influenced this model. He believed that following Prussia's humiliation by the French, a national education system would raise Germans up. This Prussian nationalism was rooted deep within his personal philosophy and was spoken of often in his lectures entitled, Addresses to the German Nation."

If you want to see the earliest beginnings of fascism, this is a great read. Not only did these lectures map out educational reform, but they also laid the groundwork for extreme nationalism. About a century later, this new approach to free and universal education would be used to generate public support of the Nazi Party.

So, the education philosophy used in the Third Reich to build up the Nazi Party was the same as the one we used to establish the foundation of our public schools in America. How interesting is that?

In Johann's lectures, he advocated the establishment of an orderly educational environment, an isolated community so to speak, that separated young students from the realities of life. The government of the schools were to be strict, using fear, intimidation, and punishment as a way to discourage disobedience, encouraging students to fall in line. Individuality and imagination were particularly discouraged, all for the sake of nationalism and knowledge.

"BY MEANS OF THE NEW EDUCATION WE WANT TO MOULD THE GERMANS INTO A CORPORATE BODY, WHICH SHALL BE STIMULATED AND ANIMATED IN ALL ITS INDIVIDUAL MEMBERS BY THE SAME INTEREST."

ADDRESS TO THE GERMAN NATION BY
JOHANN GOTTLIEB FICHTE

By the 1830s, the Prussian Model was official and running strong. Its government took the responsibility of education out of the hands of families and churches by providing free education in non-religious, government-funded buildings. Paid, professional teachers, trained in specialized schools (colleges), were well-established throughout the country; the secular curriculum was determined by, and mandated by, the Prussian national government, infused with a strong national identity.

The stated goal was to train students to be obedient, subordinate, and agreeable to all major issues. These students would grow up to be reliable factory workers, soldiers, clerks, and most importantly, obedient citizens who would be trained against questioning authority.

This was everything Horace Mann was looking for! Yes, really. The first Board of Education was created in Massachusetts with Mann as its secretary in 1837. In 1852, Massachusetts passed the compulsory education law, making school mandatory for all children. It wasn't long before the rest of the states followed suit.

And there you have it. This is the foundation of America's public school system. The bells, the scheduled classes, the tedious homework, sitting still at a desk, testing, all of these elements came from this model. The pressures of meeting established benchmarks, state standards, national standards, and a common knowledge base, all derive from the philosophies that form the basis of the Prussian Education Model—a model specifically developed with the intent of creating well-behaved citizens, subordinate to their government.

Not Reality

The format of a typical day of public school does not resemble our reality as an adult. Do you really sit in a building for eight hours a day, following rules and doing what you're told, allowing others to label you for your weaknesses and strengths, not being allowed to explore certain things that interest you? Do you wait for a bell to ring in order to be dismissed from your seat?

Okay, I get it. Some of you may. But seriously, if that does resemble your adult reality, are you happy in that environment?

Now I will say that the military is an exception. But even with its similarities, the military is a completely different—and extremely important—occupation and calling. And in all honesty, the reality of public school doesn't prepare one at all for the rigorous training one experiences in the military.

The Prussian Model of Education, as I discussed earlier, was created for an industrial age society—a society that needed lower class citizens to work in factories. They were trained through fear and intimidation to obey without question. They were taught basic education, but not too much—just enough to provide them with the tools to succeed in that environment.

The years have passed, and our society has changed, yet somehow, the public school model has not. They still hold to the philosophies of the Prussian Model.

And we wonder why our schools are failing. Do you agree with these philosophies? Or do you hold yourself to a different set of standards—a higher set of standards?

The Future of Homeschooling

Here's the truth. The future of homeschooling is whatever you want it to be. However, we must stand firm in what we believe and what we value.

It is going to be very easy for outside philosophies and ideas to leak into your home if you let them. Peer pressure is one of them, and we will discuss this in detail later. Direct or indirect government involvement within the homeschool environment is also a reality. Is this what you want for your kids?

The more you know, the more confidence you will have. In the last two chapters, I only touched on a few ideas. I have also included a list of books and documents in the Appendix that will provide you with historical information on public education. I did not go into it too much detail here, as that is not my overall goal for this book. But I felt that it might be helpful to you to know how and why our public school system is the way it is to help encourage you on your journey.

To recap, the public school system that we have today is fairly new. It is based on a Prussian model which may not agree with your personal convictions. Understanding this will unlock the freedom you deserve. Public school is not the only way. In homeschooling, we are free to choose from a myriad of educational choices.

The future of
homeschooling is
whatever you want
it to be. However,
we must stand firm
in what we believe
and what we value.

Chapter VI

Putting it in Perspective

Time Out

*B*ut first we need a time out. What did the previous chapter make you feel?

Anger? Sadness? Frustration? Encouragement? Motivation? A lot of you may be rethinking a lot of things, or perhaps just reevaluating your views on homeschooling. Well, you're not alone.

Now that you know how education has changed through the years, you should be aware that the core values of communities change, too. Leaders, government officials, and powerful people have changed the face of education without us realizing it.

And I barely touched the tip of the iceberg.

Often, we blindly follow without knowing what we're following or why.

This statement is very true when it comes to educating our kids. We just trust in the system. And even if we don't trust the system and pull them out of public/private school, we still hold on to the philosophies we were exposed to and grew up with.

For someone who went through public school as a student, this is so hard to give up. We are used to what's "normal." We've never known anything else.

But, just because it feels normal to us, that doesn't mean it's right for us—or for our children.

Spiritual Connection

As I write this, I cannot put aside God. I can't forget the impact He makes on every thought I process and every thought you process. When we view this world, we strive to look at it through His perspective—a biblical world-view. We try to view the world through His eyes. With the scriptures as our guide, we process and come to conclusions about our world and what we do.

Based on this worldview, we can conclude that the way public school is designed today is not God's design. (However, we can all agree that God can still use the public schools and that some families are called to be a part of that).

If you are called to homeschool, and you know this in your heart, He has equipped you. Put aside that man-made bondage and dwell in His freedom as you build your home with Him in mind.

Consider...

If you're homeschooling now, do you want to continue?

If you're not, would you like to start?

Do you feel as though you've made mistakes? If so, what are your thoughts on how you might correct the mistakes you feel like you've made?

How would you create a stress-free environment where your kids can learn?

If you're finding the answers to these questions hard to come by, don't worry. In the next few chapters I am going to address all of this. Together, we're going to pull it all apart, put it in perspective, and give you some ideas to help you set some solid homeschool goals that you can own. I'm going to dig deep so be prepared to change your perspective on homeschooling and your ability to be that amazing parent that can provide for your kids—provide in that way you once dreamed of as you held them in your arms for the first time.

CHAPTER VII

AM I QUALIFIED?

"HOMESCHOOLING AND PUBLIC SCHOOLING ARE AS OPPOSITE AS TWO SIDES OF A COIN. IN A HOMESCHOOLING ENVIRONMENT, THE TEACHER NEED NOT BE CERTIFIED, BUT THE CHILD MUST LEARN. IN A PUBLIC SCHOOL ENVIRONMENT, THE TEACHER MUST BE CERTIFIED, BUT THE CHILD NEED NOT LEARN."

GENE ROYER

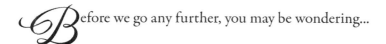 efore we go any further, you may be wondering...

Am I qualified?

There are rules in each country, in each province, in each state for homeschooling. As a citizen, you must become familiar with them. Read the actual laws, look up each word and understand what you need to do as a parent to fulfill your requirements.

This right here is the easy part. The hard part is convincing yourself that you are well-equipped to educate your kids.

I have been evaluating homeschool students in the state of Florida for more than five years. I have literally met with hundreds of families and signed off on the paperwork that allowed them to continue homeschooling. Previous to this, I taught for ten-plus years in both public and private schools. But to be completely honest, I find myself still asking myself if I am truly equipped to homeschool my kids.

We all have these thoughts, especially when we have bad days or find ourselves faced with a challenge we've never encountered before. And each challenge can be exceptionally difficult.

No amount of schooling, training, or experience can prepare you for the homeschooling parent task. But you are their parent; you will love them more than any teacher, nurse, bus driver, coach, or food-service worker.

That is one thing that qualifies you. That's what drives you.

It may sound easy, but a lot of us are still unconvinced.

Reflecting on the past and present can help some parents put things into perspective. What are the roots of public school education? Where did it come from? What does it really provide? Sure, the teachers may "know" more than you. I mean, schools offer you an entire community of well-educated, qualified specialists in their field pouring their passions into your child (hopefully) each day. But they are not you. They probably do not hold the same values as you. But what really separates you from them?

To your child, everything.

Maggie's Mom

Cindy was a homeschool mom determined to see her child succeed in whatever she wanted to succeed in. She honestly didn't expect much, especially since she herself was divorced, handicapped, and lacked a high school diploma. But at an early age, she felt convicted that bringing up her daughter in faith was more important than head knowledge.

She knew the Bible. She would lay it out every morning, carefully, and place her fingers on the worn-down letters. The sound of her daughter emptying the cereal box into the cereal bowl assured her that she was close by. Cindy's mouth would open and speak the words on her fingertips. Some of the tiny bumps had flattened a bit over the years, but Cindy knew the words by heart. Slow and steady. As she read, she could hear the crunching and the metal clashing on the side of the cereal bowl as Maggie scooped the cereal up to her mouth.

She's still here.

After a while, Cindy would engulf herself in the words she read out loud, forgetting that her daughter was near, paying attention to the God that she adored, the God that she put all her trust in. Some days she would be moved to tears, other days she would be wrapped in comfort. Not today. Today, Cindy was amazed by His faithfulness.

Eventually, the sound of a bang shook her from her trance as the empty bowl clashed to the bottom of the sink and the metal spoon echoed throughout the kitchen. Footsteps, and then silence.

She didn't even wash and dry the bowl and spoon.

But she kept reading.

After about two verses, Cindy wondered, *Is she still here? I didn't hear the chair creak or even her breathing. Did she leave the room?*

But she kept reading. Just like she always had every morning since Maggie was a baby.

She had reached the end of the chapter and slowly closed her well-loved book. A deep sigh of frustration and loneliness exited her lungs.

The only thing I'm good at is reading this book and she's not even here.

This was one of many questions running through her mind as she sat quietly in the darkness at the dining room table.

Eventually, a petite hand gently touched her arm. It frightened her a little because she didn't think anyone was there.

"Mom, I love you."

And then a sweet kiss on the check. And with that, Maggie was gone—for the moment.

What Cindy never saw was the fruit of what she had planted. Every morning, Maggie lovingly listened to her mother read scriptures. She saw how her mother trusted each word on the page and walked out her faith as the day went on. She saw her mother's perseverance, determination, character, and love. She knew no one like her mother, but like most teenage girls, she kept that part to herself.

No, Maggie did not receive the best education as some would say. She did not make A's or even B's in high school math classes like Algebra or Geometry. But she learned compassion, perseverance, and faith. That is what got her into college and graduate school. That is what pushed her to become an occupational therapist working with the handicapped, specifically the blind. No school or educational institution taught her this kind of compassion. It was her mother's influence. The influence that Cindy never thought would happen.

There are many points to this story, and each of you may get something different from it. But it is so true that the influence we have on our children goes beyond what we can see. With the right motivation, it molds them and crafts them into what they are meant to be.

Each of us is so unique.

Why on earth would any of us want to be like anyone else? Each of us has different strengths and different weaknesses, different ways of looking at the universe. It makes us who we are. So, why can't we parents focus on molding and sharpening these strengths and core values to help them succeed in specific areas unique to them?

But, what if we ourselves are uneducated? Let's be honest, you have resources galore. We have the internet, libraries, online videos, online classes, co-ops, and friends and family, each with unique perspectives and wisdom. The reality is that we have everything at our fingertips; so much so, that it's actually ridiculously overwhelming for a lot of people.

Someone once told me, "The best part of homeschooling is coming alongside my child and learning things I never knew with them."

Don't just have them read a book, read it with them. Explore nature and go on walks together. If you struggle with math, learn math with them.

But what if you don't want to teach math? You're not alone. This is when you find an app or online class that will teach them. Find a co-op or friend who would be willing to help. Just because you can't do something doesn't mean that you can't find someone or something that can teach them. Sometimes, you can't do everything. Actually, the truth is, no homeschool parent can do everything for their child. You are no superhero. You are human.

But do share with your children the things you love. Foster that love in them. While building these loving memories, you will cultivate your parent/child relationship. Nothing is more valuable. The memories that you help create will over influence any memory created in traditional school. It will stay with them forever.

You are the parent.

God Himself put you in this position.

You are qualified.

You will always be qualified.

The only thing stopping you is you.

If the desire is placed in your heart, you can homeschool. So chase after it.

We are used to what's "normal." ... But, just because it feels normal to us, that doesn't mean it's right for us— or for our children.

CHAPTER VIII

LATE TO THE GAME

There is a special kind of homeschool parent out there. They have run the race (several times), bought the book (maybe even several books), and ironically they may have written a book or two. However, nothing seems to work.

Every day is just another day. Homeschooling is just another lesson started, a lesson finished. Motivation has left the building, and all that's left is just surviving. They remember when one day in survival mode became two, and two days became a week, then a month. Eventually, it became a lifestyle, and now they're stuck. They are done.

Every morning, around 8:00am, the yellow school bus drives past their house. It's not magic, but some days it seems that way. If only. The homeschool towel is just about to be thrown in. They are tired, their kids argue with them and the only response they know is to yell back. They have run out of ideas... ideas to bring their children back to them. The only solution in their mind is to just send them away.

They have failed.

But not yet. Why? Because deep down inside there is still a twinkle of hope.

Does this sound like you?

I think all of us can relate. Even a first-year homeschooler can relate. Heck, *I* relate.

Can I Help?

There have been times that my 6-year-old has lovingly approached me during my dinner prep time asking if she could help. I look at the clock and shudder.

"No, not now. I've got to get this done."

Like all persistent children, she doesn't stop. In fact, my daughter just finds something to do next to me to make it feel like she is participating. Sometimes, she'll grab the apron and put it on. Grab her tea set or even pull up a stool and stare at me.

"Get out of the kitchen, please."

This time my words are a little more stronger, but still polite.

She looks at me with desperation in her eyes. All she wants to do is be next to me, to share in the experience, and (God forbid) learn something from me.

I told you to get out of the kitchen. I can't work like this! Do you want to eat dinner tonight? Because it's not going to happen if you keep bugging me!

My volume now has increased to a yell, my head is hot, and my tone is strong.

I am not happy.

Sometimes she stays; sometimes she listens. But eventually she runs away if I yell and threaten enough. And then I'm alone, going about my business, doing my job. Help would have been nice. It actually might possibly have made it go by quicker. We might have actually had fun together, and who cares if dinner is fifteen minutes late. Plus, maybe in the future she would have taken charge of a meal, or more. But just getting it done was what I wanted in the moment. Now the regret has crept in.

Sometimes she comes back and asks again. There is usually a second chance, or even a third. Our children always seem to come back.

I sigh, realizing I really need to engage.

"Okay, if you want to help you can set the table."

She looks at me cross-eyed.

"Setting the table is boring. I want to do what you're doing. Can I learn how to cut tomatoes? ...Pleeeease?"

See, now I have a choice. I could engage, give her what she wants, or give in to what I want.

It's true, our kids always want to come back to us. They may act like they hate us; they may yell and scream and call us bad names. But they always want to come back to us.

It doesn't matter if they are five, fifteen or twenty-five, Mom and Dad is who they want to be with. But most importantly, they want parents that want them in their lives. Parents who love them and show them love when things are good and when things are bad. They never give up on us; they are always persistent. It's human nature.

Did you ever give up on your parents?

Did they ever upset you or ignore you when you needed them the most? And you catch yourself saying, "I wish my Dad just understood me."

What would've happened if they had listened to you that one time. Let's say your best friend just moved to another city. Or, maybe, you ripped your favorite pair of pants while riding a bike.

You run to your room and slam the door loud enough for everyone to hear. But you assume no one is listening. Mom or even Dad don't care. They never care. But still you hope that the door was loud enough. That slam was your glimmer of hope; you still had faith deep down that maybe they might hear and come.

Slowly but surely, the door creaks open. Your mother's face peers through the crack. You tell her to go away, but now she doesn't listen. Instead, she sits by your side and asks you to tell her all about it.

Maybe you push her away. But she pushes back and tells you she loves you. Eventually, after the tug of war, you give in. You dig your head into her shoulder and just let out your feelings. You talk all night—about you. She listens and tells you that she understands, maybe even shares her experience and wisdom. The next thing you know, you fall asleep. Things have changed. She's your best friend—or even your hero.

Relationship First, Then Learning

Sometimes, it takes one instance like that to turn your relationship around. Maybe it takes several instances like that to turn things around. Every child is different. Every relationship is different. But it's never too late to spark that trust with them.

But, in order to homeschool successfully, you need that trust.

A lot of you may completely relate to this. Your relationship with your child is broken. The clock is ticking, soon they'll be gone and out of your home forever. Did you do the right thing? Are they prepared for life, or are you thinking, I've just got to get this done?

But truly is that where your focus is?

When you're focusing on accomplishments, when your focus is on how much information they know, how much information you can shove into their little brains, you're not considering them as a person. And more than likely, you're not cultivating a relationship with them. They are not little robots—or more appropriately, personal devices. They are people who want you and want to be loved by you first. Once this happens, learning can begin. And when this happens, learning happens faster.

But you have to be the one to change first. Yup. And honestly, you've probably heard this phrase a million times. Why? Because it's so true. And to add to that... you have to be consistent. Not just do it once or twice, but it has to be a heart change, a life change.

Our time with our children is like the time we have in the kitchen cooking. Do we send them away? Do we bark orders at them? Do we refuse to listen to the desires of their hearts, or do we let them into our world and share with them what we know how to do? Do you explore new recipes together, shop together, or even learn how to manage money together? Do you do life together?

Until you take your last breath, it's never too late. But it has to start now. Make that choice to do life with your child. Rearrange your focus and re-evaluate your goals. Now in Chapter _____ I will be discussing goal setting and how to do this successfully.

However, some of you may be thinking something totally different. When you worry about being too late, you worry that you pulled them out of school too late. They've already learned bad educational habits. Let's talk about this in the next chapter.

But super-quick, if you've ever heard of de-schooling, this is what it is: putting aside curricula and academics to focus on your relationship and develop trust with your kids. Even homeschool parents need to de-school from homeschool. Especially when they notice the stress tension and unhealthy struggles. De-schooling can happen over a month, a day, or even a year. We will definitely talk about that later, but first....

...let's talk about academics.

CHAPTER IX

I'M DONE WITH THIS

"I'm done with this! The teachers don't listen to me, my child is failing, my son is made fun of because of his disability. What has this world come to?"

Candace said this to herself as she huffed and puffed her way out of a parent-teacher conference early Monday morning. Tears flooded her eyes as she fumbled through her purse for her car keys.

The thought of homeschooling has been on her mind for quite a while. In fact, while her son was at school she would research local co-ops, watch YouTube videos, and read blogs about homeschooling. She knew she could totally jump the train.

The night before, she and her husband had *the talk*.

"It's time," he said. "I believe in you. If anyone can do it, you can. Tomorrow, withdraw him from school and then take him out to celebrate."

"But maybe they can do better. Isn't that what they're trained to do?" Candace protested.

She vividly remembers the impact her teachers had made on her when she was young, how she was able to excel to the top of the class because their influence was so strong. Maybe they could do the same for her son? Or, maybe it was just too late.

49

She stopped in her tracks in the middle of the parking lot. She stood still and exhaled, watching her breath fade away in the cold morning air. As she breathed a second time, she composed herself. Slowly, she turned around and began the long walk back to the main door of the school office. She didn't know if she was shivering from the cold or from her nerves, but she knew what she needed to do.

And she did.

Within moments, her son's hand was in hers, and all of his curriculum, books and schoolmates were left behind within the icy doors of the school building.

They both walked boldly to the car. Her key ignited the engine and their new journey began.

Within weeks, she had her son, Matthew, tested with two different standardized tests. She had him reevaluated and was able to get him more therapy sessions. She enrolled him in two co-ops and became involved in another social co-op.

Yet, disappointment was all she could see.

His test scores placed him two levels below in math. His language arts was behind, and so was his general knowledge. He already expressed how overwhelmed he was from all the classes he was enrolled in at the co-op. He didn't want to work. And to top it off, when she told him that he would have to do two lessons of math a day just to catch up, he had a meltdown. How on earth was she going to catch him up?

As she sat on the couch and wept, her only thought was, *How am I ever going to do this? I'm too late! I should have started homeschooling long ago. I have failed him!*

With every time she spoke these words in her mind, came more tears. And every time she took a breath, guilt wrapped its way around her heart.

Where Do You Go Now?

The first problem here is what she was putting her faith in. Those scores, those therapies, the grades, his reactions, other people's opinions about what her child has (or hasn't) accomplished. These things only clouded her vision of the truth.

The truth is, she was relying on public school standards and benchmarks and what they were saying about who her child was. She was using them as a way to measure her son against something. If he could accomplish those goals set out by the system, then he was succeeding. If he couldn't, then he was a failure.

Have you ever been to the doctor and find yourself angry and frustrated. Let's say you walk in with a sore throat. They run tests, check your temperature, and then prescribe a bunch of medicine. Why? Because that's what the books told the doctor to do. Instead of examining and understanding the person and where they were physically and emotionally, they just followed the rules. They were rude. They didn't listen and they came across as knowing it all. In our home, we call that 'no bedside manner.' Well, I believe that's how our children feel sometimes.

Instead of treating the *person*, they were treating the *problem*. In fact, *all they see* is the problem.

That is what happened with Candace and Matthew. And for a lot of parents, they look at the problem instead of the child. Matthew is failing Math, Joannah can't score higher than 800 on her SATs. Sarah just failed 4th grade.

This could be considered by some as a problem.

But what about the *person*?

What about slowing down and understanding why a child is having a problem, where the child is stumbling. Maybe it's a disability. Maybe it's misunderstanding, or maybe it's self-esteem. But the only way to find that out is through relationships, through a gentle, positive relationship, not a forced relationship. And forcing curriculum and books on children, especially when they don't want that, is the worst thing you can do.

But also note, sometimes they were not built to excel in math. Maybe, memorizing the dates to each battle of the American Civil War is just incredibly boring to them. This is all okay.

Every child is different.

The second problem lies with a lack of understanding the philosophy behind homeschooling and the local homeschool laws. Sometimes, the only way to do this is to meet with a seasoned homeschool family, go to conferences and events, get involved with co-ops, read state requirements, and see a homeschooler in action first-hand.

Once Candace understood homeschooling, that she had the freedom to take her time, pick her own curriculum, and do what she needed to do to help her son, the pressure slowly came off. In fact, she was able to teach him for an extra year so he could catch up and graduate.

A Sparkle of Hope

Eventually, Candace did regroup. It took some convincing and a lot of talking, but being teachable really helped. Being present for her son was Number One. Then, setting aside the pressures and expectations was next. She was also in a unique situation. Her son had ADHD and was slightly on the spectrum. Understanding more about his disability, listening to him, and understanding things from his perspective were huge milestones in accomplishing their homeschool goals. And all of this didn't happen overnight. It took love and patience.

Eventually, Candance was also able to understand that she wasn't at fault. And even though Matthew's memories of school were awful, he didn't blame her. In fact, his mom became his hero. The past was the past and the present was glorious. Now, with her husband, they were able to pour love and compassion into their son.

I'll be honest. Matthew never excelled in math, but that was to be expected. Once Candace and her husband accepted that, things became a lot easier for them as they schooled him. In fact, if you ask them today, they would tell you that it wouldn't have made a difference if they had started homeschooling him earlier.

He did graduate Homeschooling High School, and now he is truly enjoying his work in the restaurant business. He is kind, he is respectful, and has a servant's heart. His parents taught him all of this.

A Parent's Influence

My father always taught me...

It doesn't matter what you do with your life. As long as you enjoy what you do, that's what matters.

You could be the most cunning lawyer in the world or the most skilled heart surgeon, if it stresses you out, if it brings misery to your life and you hate it... you're not successful.

But if you simply work in retail, wait tables, or park people's cars and you enjoy the work, it pays the bills, and as a bonus you even enjoy the people who work with you, then you're successful.

We need every kind of person. People to design roads, people to keep track of the finances, and people to build the roads. No one job is more important than another.

What does matter, though, is how you treat people, your values, and the relationships you build with people. Those are the things that follow you through life. Those are the things that help you attain your goals, help you handle bad situations better, and give you a positive outlook on life. No one remembers you for your ACT and SAT scores. No one cares if you graduated with honors. What they do care about is how you treat them.

Sometimes, taking an extra month or year to focus on character building is worth its weight in gold. And yes, some parents do that and it is 100% justifiable. Think about yourself. What if you spent one year of your life focusing on character building, learning how to treat people with respect? Your homework could include opening doors for people, following the interruption rule properly, learning how to listen attentively, visiting the elderly, service projects, missionary trips, delivering meals for the sick, babysitting for free, and even making crafts and cards for the lonely. Would you learn that there's an entire world of people who need love? Would you stop focusing on what needs to be done and more on how it needs to be done? Would you learn empathy and compassion? How would all of this affect who you are?

Deschooling

Deschooling is a real thing. Some believe that every parent should do it immediately after withdrawing their child from traditional school. Some don't. However, it is an option someone can take if you just need that time to connect: mother to child, father to child.

When you deschool, you literally put all types of academics aside and just focus on living life together as a family, giving each other time to forgive, mend the broken pieces, and grow closer together. Once you feel you're ready, you can gradually move into simple stuff. Maybe you begin learning about nature together or try some science experiments. Maybe you sit down and read a good book together or even visit a history museum. It gives the parents time to get to know their children and time to pick out a proper curriculum. It gives them time to discover their philosophies on education and even time to write out some goals.

Deschooling can also be suggested for parents who came out of the traditional school system. And I'm going to say honestly that deschooling should definitely happen for parents who are former teachers. In fact, they probably need it more than anyone. I can say that because I had to deschool... several times.

Overall, it's just a nice time of reflection and relationship building, setting everything aside, taking a break and focusing on each other.

Now, after all of this talk about deschooling, accepting the task of educating and grabbing hold of your freedoms in education, we need to discuss how you will address their needs and set them up for success. How are you going to take what's important and set up some goals for your homeschool? Deschooling is a real thing. Some believe that every parent should do it immediately after withdrawing their child from traditional school. Some don't. However, it is an option someone can take if you just need that time to connect: mother to child, father to child.

When you deschool, you literally put all types of academics aside and just focus on living life together as a family, giving each other time to forgive, mend the broken pieces, and grow closer together. Once you feel you're ready, you can gradually move into simple stuff. Maybe you begin learning about nature together or try some science experiments. Maybe you sit down and read a good book together or even visit a history museum. It gives the parents time to get to know their children and time to pick out a proper curriculum. It gives them time to discover their philosophies on education and even time to write out some goals.

Deschooling can also be suggested for parents who came out of the traditional school system. And I'm going to say honestly that deschooling should definitely happen for parents who are former teachers. In fact, they probably need it more than anyone. I can say that because I had to deschool... several times.

Overall, it's just a nice time of reflection and relationship building, setting everything aside, taking a break and focusing on each other.

Now, after all of this talk about deschooling, accepting the task of educating and grabbing hold of your freedoms in education, we need to discuss how you will address their needs and set them up for success. How are you going to take what's important and set up some goals for your homeschool?

CHAPTER X

SETTING THEM UP FOR SUCCESS

*J*ennifer had three daughters.

She loved all of them equally.

And all of them were very different.

Katie was the youngest, and she had spunk. She was always into everything. She took apart watches, alarm clocks, computers, even kitchen appliances, trying to figure out how they worked and how she might improve their function. Katie drove her mom absolutely crazy. Parts were always laying around the kitchen, under the couch, and even the bathroom. Worst of all, Jennifer had no ideas what to do with these parts or what appliance or gizmo they might belong to.

For Katie, Jennifer decided to focus on her interests. This meant that she was involved with the homeschool robotics team, really studied up on physics and math classes, and even got an internship in her field while still in high school. She was self-motivated to go to college. Jennifer didn't have much to worry about when it came to Katie's future.

The next daughter was Addison. Addison had no idea what she wanted to do with her life. She was more of a "go with the flow" type of child. No dreams, no goals, nothing that gave much of a clue to what she enjoyed— except for her love of being social. In her case, Jennifer just gave her basic school assignments and was thankful when Addison paid attention during family discussions. She did, however, pose a lot of, "How you should treat people" questions to her, and etiquette training, as well. They also talked through a lot of drama and what might be the best method for handling each situation. This was the majority of Addison's schooling.

And then there was Tracy. The world revolved around Tracy; not just because she was the oldest but because she was who the family had put so much time and money into. Tracy's schooling revolved around her hobby. She was going to be an Olympic athlete.

Every morning at 5 am, she woke up, ate breakfast, and began her training at the pool. Lap after lap, breath after breath. The one thing that kept her going was the hope that the whole world one day would be watching her. As Tracy glided through the water, she imagined stands filled with people rooting for her, supporting her, and cheering her on.

She would make her way home around 9 am, dripping wet. Casually raiding the refrigerator, Tracy would walk around in her swimsuit, as comfortably as if it were casual wear. After a quick snack, she spent some time studying, but was quick enough to make it back to practice by noon. This was her life, every day.

She studied the basics. Nothing advanced, only the things she needed to have in order to qualify for certain sporting events that she needed to prove her schooling to. But the basics were all she did. Math, language arts, science, and history were it. And, honestly, she had no interest in them. Education was to get her from Point A to Point B. Swimming was her thing.

Jennifer knew that Tracy would eventually be a swim coach or instructor, and because of that, college would be something to talk about. She kept a close watch on that. But truly, her Olympic dreams were where Tracy's focus was.

Jennifer admits that all her kids were easy to educate. They all had different personalities and required different classes, approaches, training, and academics. But she focused on what they individually needed. Yes, they did have family time with the Bible, and even science or history discussions.

But for the most part, each one required their own unique set of instructions. Why? Because each one needed an individual approach in order for them to succeed in what they were created to be.

There is no one set way that any homeschool parent is required to teach. Homeschooling, unlike public school, is not dead-set on making cookie-cutter society members. You have the power, the qualifications—and most importantly—the right to provide what is necessary for your child. That can be anywhere from social skills classes for a son with autism to swim lessons for a future medalist. It could be teaching your kids how to care for pets to allowing them to open an online store to sell bracelets. You are providing opportunities for them.

But what about the basic academics? What do they need to learn?

As an evaluator, I get this question a lot. Yes, some regions or states lay this out for you, but some do not. But, even though the majority of parents tend to agree on what the basics are, you're not married to these. Nor are you limited to these.

The top three are (suggested by many parents):

Math

Reading

Writing

The "three Rs" as they used to call them.

I hesitate to give you this suggestion, but I will add that this is very good advice. You can even think of it as sound direction—a good starting place. Maybe, even, the bare minimum.

Math is a core subject. You need this to make accurate calculations, read clocks, plan events, know when to show up to places, know how far something is, and of course, go shopping. You can't go shopping without math.

Reading is a core subject. This was one subject our forefathers really wanted to see everyone be able to do. You need reading to vote, to shop online or at a store, get into college, gather information, read the Bible, and of course, engross yourself in great literature.

Writing is also a core subject. This not only includes the basic ability to write letters but includes story writing, spelling and even grammar. Writing is a form of communication. We do this online, through social media, email, and even if we go "old school" and write a letter.

There are so many other subjects and topics to choose from. Everything from science and history to foreign languages and music. What's even more fun is when you can combine them. For example, you can read about Native American Indians and learn about their culture, then go on a field trip to a museum, and even write papers on what you've learned. You could do this with anything; there is no limitation.

Another fun thing to do is focus on one topic within a subject: American government, ancient history, marine biology, reptiles, etc. These are called unit studies, and many kids love to learn this way. It absorbs them into a subject, and instead of it being just a brief overview, they can really dive deep into it since the basics are fresh on their minds.

Don't Get Too Advanced

Another important tip is to not get too advanced for them. Don't teach over their heads.

Of all the mistakes a homeschool mom can make, this was mine.

With my first-born son, I was eager, excited, and full of fun ideas. The only problem was, I wanted to teach him higher level ideas. I knew that younger kids were sponges and my plan was to take advantage of that.

When he was in kindergarten, I purchased a unit study curriculum on Africa. I was convinced that he was going to learn and memorize every country on the continent of Africa. Then he was going to make a map and recite them. Everyone would clap. He would be the smartest kid ever.

We spent every day drawing maps and reciting names. (Honestly, I did most of the work.) He did color the map though. I will give him that.

So much stress and anxiety went into it. I drilled him on each country, including the correct pronunciation. Then he had to tell me a little about each one, what language they spoke, or what their homes looked like. That kind of stuff.

At the end of study, he did have his map (which I ended up making) and I hung it proudly on the wall. (Yes, I had him recite the countries to friends and family when they stopped by.)

But in the end... guess what?

He doesn't know the name of any countries in Africa, except South Africa, Egypt, Morocco, Congo, Kenya, and Djibouti (and yes, it's because it's way too fun to say... especially since he's now in middle school).

And he hates the idea of tracing maps. He always has. Now, might this be because I pushed him into doing it? I don't know. But either way, hindsight being 20/20, it was not very fun, interesting, or fruitful. Maybe, one would say, it was a waste of time.

What should I have done?

If I were granted a do-over, I would have focused on what interested him. In his case, he loved outer space. I would have spent that time singing songs about planets, reading and looking through books on the topic, doing coloring pages, and even molding some papier mâché balloons to place around the entire room. I would have allowed him to paint each planet with the appropriate color, however he liked. Messy, neat, didn't matter because it would be done outside. I would join in and just enjoy talking about them, sharing fun facts, and slowing down.

That's the key, slowing down and enjoying what you have in front of you. That's how you build those memories—not with pushing facts and terms into their brains, but allowing the experience to make an eternal memory in their mind. And also, remaining committed.

Whenever you pick a topic or subject, it's so important that you stick with it. You repeat it. You remind them. Otherwise, they forget it. That's why you practice reading every single day, counting every single day. That's why you have to practice a language in order to remember it.

If I had made my son recite the name of every country in Africa every day for several years, it would now be ingrained in his mind. But I will admit that, at the time, it didn't feel like it was worth it. I wasn't committed.

Now, as is always the case, there are exceptions to the rule. Sometimes, you pick a topic, a subject, or a curriculum and they're just not ready for it. Or, it may not be an interest for them. Or even worse, it's something that doesn't fit their learning style.

Learning Styles

I love all the charts on learning styles. There are so many. But I can't move on until I share some.

Here are the top three—plus a bonus one:

The *Visual Learner* learns with charts, graphs, movies, photos, anything they can see.

The *Auditory Learner* learns from recordings, podcasts, audiobooks, lectures, anything they can hear.

The *Kinesthetic Learner* learns through experience, activities, experiments, games, anything they can get directly involved with.

And the bonus one is the *Reading and Writing Learner*. This learner learns from books, blogs, writing in their journal, writing summaries, anything involving words on a page (physical or on a computer).

Most of you know these, and you also know that your child's learning style is super important. Also, knowing your own learning style is important since most of the time this is how you enjoy teaching—and most kids do take after their parents. I want to encourage you to go online, take a learning style test, take a test for your child, and start there. Find opportunities that will help them learn more easily.

As an added bonus, I love Gardner's Multiple Intelligence Chart. This is not limited to learning; it also shows how a person expresses themselves, how they perform, and how they learn, remember, and understand things. Of course, it can overlap, too. You can belong to one category or several.

This is just a good reminder that we are all so different and unique. It reminds us that we don't need to be fit into a box, that we shouldn't be comparing our kids to others. You should be who you were meant to be—and so should your kids.

Now, with that said, check out these categories...

Visual—Spatial: These are your future fashion designers, interior decorators, architects, and navigators. They like to draw, do puzzles, read maps, give directions, and even daydream. They are aware of their surroundings, how things are placed, and they remember things this way.

This fits one of my sons. He enjoys studying maps, getting to know our city, the street names, building cities out of LEGOs, and rearranging his room. In fact, he's the one who is best able to give me directions when I get lost.

They learn well with graphs, charts, drawings, models, videos, television, and other multimedia sources.

Body—Kinesthetic: These are your costume designers, dancers, athletes, and yes... surgeons. They like movement, making things, and touching things. They can be very expressive with their body and hands. They're very physical, and can even be a bit too hands-on.

After talking to one of my daughter's doctors, he described her possible surgeon as an artist. He said that when this surgeon works on the heart, it's like nothing he's ever seen. He is completely aware of every working part, aware of what his hands and arms are doing, and he can reconstruct it like no one else. No textbook can teach you this.

These people learn through roleplay, physical activities, movement, hands-on learning, and experiences.

Musical: These are your musicians, conductors, or anyone who uses sound to do their job. This can include car mechanics, air traffic controllers, and audio engineers. They pay attention to subtleties of sound, through music, rhythm, or even tone.

A friend of mine was gifted at telling you exactly what was wrong with your car as soon as you turned it on. Each squeal, the rhythm of the engine, loudness, softness, each sound told him what part was working properly and what part needed to be checked.

These learners learn best with music, poetry, tapping, instruments, or auditory media.

Interpersonal: This is understanding, interacting with others. These students learn through interaction. They have many friends, empathy for others, street smarts. They can be taught through group activities, seminars, dialogues. Tools include the telephone, audio conferencing, time and attention from the instructor, video conferencing, writing, computer conferencing, and E-mail.

Intrapersonal: This is understanding one's own interests, one's personal goals. These learners tend to shy away from others. They're in tune with their inner feelings; they have wisdom, intuition, and motivation, as well as a strong will, confidence, and opinions. They can be taught through independent study and introspection. Tools include books, creative materials, diaries, privacy, and time. They are the most independent of the learners.

Linguistic: This is using words effectively. These learners have highly-developed auditory skills and often think in words. They like reading, playing word games, making up poetry or stories. They can be taught by encouraging them to say and see words, read books together. Tools include computers, games, multimedia, books, tape recorders, and lectures.

Logical—Mathematical: This is reasoning, calculating. These people think conceptually, abstractly and are able to see and explore patterns and relationships. They like to experiment, solve puzzles, ask cosmic questions. They can be taught through logic games, investigations, mysteries. They need to learn and form concepts before they can deal with details.

Did any of these stick out as you? As your child? Did a couple of them seem to fit? Did it explain why you do certain things or have certain superhuman abilities? These are cool, huh?

But seriously, when you know your style as well as your child's style, you can filter everything through these. You can get super creative, too.

CHAPTER XI

LET'S TALK COLLEGE

In the Mind of a Homeschool Graduate

"Everything is so silly," Rebecca said to me suddenly. I had just asked her how college was going. "It's all about numbers and grades and awards. I get college. I get why I go and I honestly love it, but sometimes... it's just different. They do things differently. But the crazy part is, it's so easy. Actually, I think it's making me lazy. I don't have to read the whole book anymore."

She continued.

"For example, the first week of school the professors spent a great amount of time putting us in our place. Lecture after lecture about how we needed to work hard and earn their respect. There was no free ride, our mommies weren't going to save us. So, I was stressed and scared. I spent hours studying only to find that I didn't need to. It's like a cake walk. But the other students, I don't get it. They're struggling."

Rebecca was your typical self-motivated homeschooler. Math was her strong suit and she wanted to be a computer programmer. Academic would be a great word to describe her. She knew what she believed, why she did what she did, and did the research to prove it.

Now, Sally was in college, too. She was an artist—an artist with words. Foreign lands and worlds swirled in her mind that no one on earth had ever explored, and she knew that she was good at it. Getting into college was easy, but because her math scores were on the lower end, scholarships were scarce.

"Some of my friends are doing so well, they get awards and scholarships, and I'm so proud of them." At this, she looked down, "But I know that as jealous as I may get, this won't last forever. Those awards mean nothing in the grand scheme of things. In the end, we will both have a degree."

Two different types of homeschoolers experiencing the reality of the schooling mindset.

Nowadays, colleges cater to the mentality of a former public school student. They want success from them, and sometimes awards, competition, and scholarships feed their ego and push them to do better.

"The higher the numbers and scores, the more money they make," one homeschool college student said to me. "I just want to focus on my craft and get better at it. I don't really care about that stuff."

Homeschoolers do succeed. But sometimes, they think differently. A lot of them are more mature, they see the big picture, some find college boring, some don't go to college at all.

The beautiful thing about homeschooling is that they are all different. Every child is unique and brings so much variety to this world. They have unique perspectives on life.

One thing I notice is that, because they have such a strong support group of friends and family, their confidence level is pretty high. By not going to school, they bypass the harsh bullying, unnecessary competition, and pressure. Now, of course there's some, it's not eliminated completely, but it isn't present to the degree that we see it in schools.

Homeschoolers in College

According to The Princeton Review, there are specific things that colleges look at when deciding which applicants will be admitted.

1) High school transcripts, GPA, the kinds of classes that were taken, whether the applicant was sufficiently challenged, and standardized test scores (which would be ACT and SAT scores), and the college essay, which can be as unique as each applicant. You'll want this to stand out!

2) Recommendation letters. As a homeschooler family you know some pretty cool people. People with integrity and influence.

3) Demonstrative Interest. All the stuff they love, all the stuff they spend unassigned time doing. Yup!

4) List of Extracurricular Activities. This can include archery, piano, dramatics, Boy Scouts, novel writing, volunteer work, bill writing, etc... What's great about homeschooling is we sometimes have more time to do this.

But this is basic. Every college is slightly different, and it's good to know what those differences are. Whenever I go to evaluate a high-schooler, I always recommend calling the college admissions counselor to ask for specifics; and I personally recommend doing this as soon as they enter 9th grade so that there will be no surprises.

But what do colleges really look for?

A few years ago, I had the privilege of casually chatting with a college admissions counselor. One of my questions was, "What do colleges think of homeschoolers?"

"You would be surprised," he said. "Colleges love homeschoolers, and I'll tell you why: Their outlook and philosophies about education are beyond the typical public, and even the typical private, school student. They realize that going to college is a privilege and not a requirement. Going to college is something that they want to do, not something that they're forced into by their parents and peers.

"They stand out because they actually love learning. They mostly go above and beyond what the professors ask; they are eager and curious. Because of this, their overall GPA is higher and the dropout rate is extremely low. Colleges hate dropouts. We lose money. Homeschoolers help us make money, let's be honest.

But they have integrity, they're polite, they're reliable and dedicated. That's the impression we have of them, and we're usually right. So, when I see an application from a homeschooler come across my desk, I put it in a special pile. But, believe me when I tell you this, I'm not the only one. We're not the only college that thinks this way. This is nationwide."

This was the most encouraging thing I had ever heard, since it wasn't what I expected from the college perspective.

But What if They Don't Want to Go?

There are many homeschoolers who don't want to go to college. It's not required, it's not demanded, or maybe it's just not their thing—so they don't go.

When this happens, our old philosophies and expectations as parents may come out, those philosophies that our parents, and our parents' parents, ingrained in us, pressured us with. It can make us feel guilty, like we failed them, and we beat ourselves up over it.

When I was young, it was just expected. When I graduated from high school, I remember going from one graduation party to the next, and the colleges they were going to attend was always at the forefront of each conversation. I even went to a high school graduation party themed as the college. It's just what was done, the progression of life.

I even remember how, at my high school graduation, as each student came up to receive their diploma, the college they were going to was announced. I remember being somewhat ashamed that I was just going to our local community college. It was by choice, yet I was still ashamed, and I felt like I had to constantly justify my reasons.

I think our society has relaxed a bit now. College is not always expected. Some people are gifted with working with their hands, they inherit a family business, or they want to jump in and start their own business. Others just need a break to ground themselves, and of course, there's the highest calling of all: parenting. Some women (and men, too) find that they just want to raise their children and be a homemaker. We need all types of people and workers because we are all so different and unique.

It's so tempting to be disappointed in yourself as a parent. But don't be. Remember, we're here to guide them into becoming who they're meant to be. There's a plan for them, and not everyone is college-bound. That doesn't mean that you shouldn't encourage them. What it means is that you should encourage them with wisdom to pursue the things they'll enjoy doing and the things that they're good at.

My dad always said to me, "I don't care what you do with your life, as long as you do what you love. If you do something that you don't love, you'll be miserable." And he was right.

Very patiently, he allowed me to pursue theatre, dance, and music. He paid for my dance lessons, singing lessons, and acting classes for many, many years. I eventually realized that it wasn't my thing to do professionally, and instead I pursued teaching. Not because I wasn't good at theater, I just didn't want to do it anymore. I fell in love with the idea of teaching, and even now I miss it. There's nothing in the world like it; but see, it's my thing.

Yes, I had to have a college degree for this, as with many other careers in the world. But not everyone needs to go to college to be who God designed them to be.

Parents do have wisdom, and at this time in your life, when your homeschooler is about to graduate from high school, you need to stop listening to the trends, the expectations, the pressures. You know your child better than anyone. God has given you the wisdom to raise them, no one else has.

So, chat with your spouse and/or pray. Talk with your homeschooler with open ears and encouraging words. This should not be anyone's agenda; they are not a creature that you can manipulate. They have choices, and if they don't choose college, understand why, and find ways to encourage them on the journey they choose.

Allowing your kids to fly, to soar, is one of the hardest things a parent has to do (besides labor, just saying). But it's something we have to do. Have patience, and trust.

Will others judge you? I'm sure they will; there will always be critics. But don't let that get you down. You need to have confidence so that you can have confidence in your children. They need your encouragement and support along the way or they will have trouble succeeding in being who they were meant to be.

Now as a parent, I mentioned, God gives you wisdom. That is so true. And you can share that wisdom. You have had experiences, you understand the world better, so don't be afraid to give them direction and advice.

But check yourself. The worst thing you can do is to give them advice from a selfish motive. Wanting them to go to college because that's what's expected is selfish. Wanting them to go to college because you notice that they're fascinated with laws, with speech and debate, and have expressed interest in becoming a lawyer, that's not selfish. With words of encouragement, you can put a fire under them like no one can, with confidence-building words, and by having belief that they can do it.

I encourage you to think about this a bit. It can get complicated, but it's simple. To sum up, check your motives, trust your instincts, pray, and be positive.

To share with you my story, my father knew that I was going to be a teacher because he knew me. Through my high school career pursuing performing arts and on through college, he would briefly mention that I would be a very good teacher. How he knew this, I don't know. It could have been the many times I set up a classroom with my dolls with my sister, wrote tests, my love for education, for learning, for talking about things, I don't know.

But he knew. And it was easy for me to pursue. He encouraged me. He also, in my later years, encouraged me to start a YouTube channel and write this book. He always said, "I know you, and I know you would love this."

And he was right.

Don't ever underestimate the wisdom of a parent! We know things.

Setting Goals

*N*ow that you have some perspective, let's get down to business, because homeschool isn't always fun and games. Okay, it can be, but there is work to be done. And when there is work, there are usually goals that need to be met.

But mostly, I stress setting goals because it's so easy to slip back into bad habits. With a fresh perspective and a renewed motivation, you need to set these goals. Through the year, or however long you set them for, you will experience all sorts of bumps and falls. These goals you set will keep you focused. And these goals, by the way, are your goals.

But why set homeschool goals?

When we set goals, we set ourselves up for long-term success. Our eyes become focused on that accomplishment and we pursue it every day. Every day that you reach that goal, you succeed, and it motivates you to do it again and again.

In order to achieve that goal, however, you have to be disciplined. You have to be able to organize your thoughts and resources in order to make it long term. If you are passionate about your goals, you will get so much out of it.

But the key is to be passionate.

As a parent, we have the chance to influence a person more than anyone else. We can share our values and passions, and they will grab a hold of it. Sometimes, without question. Why not focus this positively? Why not utilize your time and set purposeful goals?

What do they look like?

Goals can be anything. Anything you find value in.

For many people, including me, faith is a huge value. It's even the foundation upon which everything in our lives is built and we hinge our entire homeschooling on it. With a foundation and core value so large, you can easily pull several goals from it.

- Finding a faith-based curriculum.

- Reading scripture for 30 minutes a day with everyone.

- Getting involved in faith-based community outreaches once a month.

More than likely, you will never find these goals in a public school.

One of my goals is to read one book aloud with my kids every month. Sitting with my kids, reading the story, and imagining it playing out in their heads, brings me great joy. And beyond that, discussing the morals and facets of each book gives me so much insight into who they are and how they think. Not only does it build critical thinking and develop a love for reading, it also brings families closer together. We share an experience together. I love it, they love it, and we all benefit from it.

Spending quality time with my family is one of my core values.

About five years ago, I had a goal of purchasing season passes to Disney World and visiting the parks with my kids each week. Yes, this was one of my homeschooling educational goals. Last year, we were able to do this.

Leadership is a quality that my son possesses. At home, he built cities out of LEGOs, wrote out rules and organized governments that the little LEGO people had to obey. Even though he was only two inches tall, King Isaac ruled with compassion and fairness.

As my son grew, his curiosity for structure and how people could help keep order has led him to a love of history. Unlike many children, he is fascinated by the study of government. He has studied the U.S. Constitution and has an opinion on many past presidents. Some have become heroes. One of them is Abraham Lincoln.

"Best president ever!" he boldly proclaimed while waiting in line for the American Adventure at EPCOT. The echo of his voice rang loud and clear. It was an understatement to say that many thought it was adorable. And I was proud.

Walking through the interior of the building, with its rotunda featuring singers bringing the beginnings of America to life with their voices, put Isaac into a daze. While this was happening, my other son, Ethan, wandered off into the small Native American Museum.

"Wow, Mom! Look at this!"

It was a musical instrument made from animal guts. "Do you think it actually worked? I bet I could make one."

By the time the singers finished and it was our turn to go into the theater, we were pretty well-known. I mean, who else brings kids to Disney in the middle of the week in February? Needless to say, my kids led the way. They pointed at flags as we went up the elevator.

"Do you know why that flag has only thirteen stars?" I asked.

"Yes, the thirteen colonies!"

"And does that one have more stars because it has more states?"

"Yes, sir."

Proud mom in the building. And it didn't end there.

During the 30-minute show, my kids were full of questions and ah-ha moments, from Susan B. Anthony to Theodore Roosevelt, who is my daughter's favorite president because of his work with the national parks. Their seat did not stay warm, except for the very edge, because that's where they sat.

As the show drew to a close, Mark Twain spoke this famous line:

> "WE NOW FACE THE DANGER, WHICH IN THE PAST HAS BEEN THE MOST DESTRUCTIVE TO THE HUMANS: SUCCESS, PLENTY, COMFORT, AND EVER-INCREASING LEISURE. NO DYNAMIC PEOPLE HAS EVER SURVIVED THESE DANGERS."

As we exited, I repeated this line to my kids. "What does this mean?"

Needless to say, the conversation continued as we walked to our next destination. And to this day, my oldest son can explain the truth behind this statement.

This was one little moment that helped motivate him to learn more about history, government, and even politics. His current ambition is to become a politician and maybe even President.

But this was just one moment from many moments we experienced that year.

Not many people realize how much education can happen on these "field trips." We made it a point to slowly experience each section and each attraction one at a time. We once read *Tom Sawyer* on Tom Sawyer's Island. We traveled around the world at Epcot with a map of each country and talked with the employees about their homes and culture. We learned about Walt Disney, his upbringing and how he chased his dreams and never gave up.

They attended a drawing session. They learned about animals at Animal Kingdom one country at a time. The list goes on.

Learning with your hands does stimulate long-term memories. You can associate smells with colors and touch with sound. Their senses are fully engaged and learning is at its best. To this day, my kids can tell you how to keep manatees safe, or how Japan and China are different. They can even explain how magnets can be used to make a theme park attraction work, because they were inspired to research this on their own. *Physics!* They learned this at Disney World.

Let's Get Started

Here are some reflections to help you find your goals. Remember this is a starting point. And these questions are here for you to brainstorm ideas. Also remember to include your spouse if possible. They should always have a 50/50 say in your child's education. In fact, I would encourage you to answer these questions together over dinner or coffee.

What's Important for You and Your Family

Focus on your family and your values. Don't think about others or what you think they want you to think or do. This includes the public schools and benchmarks. Don't let them influence you in these thoughts. What's important for *your* family? What are *your* values? Some can be educational and some can just reflect relationships.

Write down as many as you can.

Achievable Goals

Make sure your goals can be achieved. For example, you may have a value that says you want your kids to learn a musical instrument. Now set it to something achievable:

By the end of this week, they'll pick out an instrument and we'll purchase it. Then he'll start music lessons by the end of next week.

Family time is important. That's a great value. Now set some achievable goals:

We will go out once a week to some kind of family activity. We will purchase museum passes to go monthly.

The list can go on. Write a few of these goals down.

What do you enjoy doing?

Write down at least five things that you enjoy doing. These can be hobbies or jobs. Then later, reflect on how and if they might help you achieve your above goals.

For example, I love to rollerblade. Can I use this hobby as a tool to reach a goal? Sure! We can rollerblade together to bring our family together. We can talk and skate. We can even enjoy nature and explore the outdoors on a rollerblading trip.

Set Small Goals

Reflect on some of your goals from above. Do you have any small, quick goals? These are always good to have because they are super easy, and once you accomplish them, you feel motivated to do another.

A checklist is a great way to set small goals, like, *They will finish their project by the end of this week.* Or, *They will be able write a page in cursive within twenty minutes.* Also, feel free to creatively incorporate your hobbies.

Add anything you wish to add now.

Break Up the Large Goals

You may have written that you want to read through the Bible with your family in a year. Break this up into smaller goals, like, *This week we will read Chapters 1 – 30 of Genesis. Today, we will read Chapters 1 - 5.* Accomplishing these little goals will combine to accomplish big goals, and sometimes you don't realize how far you've come until the end.

Break up some of your larger goals mentioned above.

Deadlines

Deadlines keep you motivated and give you something to look forward to. Make sure that your goals include a deadline.

Your Next Step

By this time, you should have some goals in mind. This is great! Write them down. I've included some extra pages in the back to get you started. Or even better, start a goal journal. Whatever it takes to have them in writing.

Now, in the next chapter I've written out some of the most popular homeschooling philosophies and some of the most popular curricula within each philosophy. This is not an end-all, be-all. Honestly, use this as a guide, as an arrow pointing you toward a fulfilling direction. Some of you may find, however, that one or two philosophies click with you. Feel free to dive in. Some of you may find that none of these methods fit your family's views on education. That's okay, too. Feel free to make up your own. But let's just touch on some of these philosophies now.

Chapter XIII

An Abridged Discussion of Homeschooling Philosophies

*I*t would be so easy for me to write an entire book on homeschooling philosophies, but that is not my purpose here. However, when you're setting goals and finding ways to meet them, understanding what your homeschooling philosophy is, can really push you in the right direction.

Below are the most popular philosophies. You may find one of them to be completely your style. Maybe two. Maybe even all of them. Some may find that none of these describe their philosophy, and that's totally okay, too.

The point is that these philosophies will help you find support quickly and easily, curricula that are likely to work well for you, and groups of like-minded people. Honestly, it will make your decision making a lot less stressful.

And, as always, be flexible. You may dive into one of these only to find that it isn't you and your family's philosophy at all. It happens more than you think. Just go back to the drawing board and reevaluate your goals and ideas. And of course, you can always use this chapter as a reference.

The Traditional Method

With this philosophy you believe that a student learns best through memorization and recitation. The tools and methods used most are: textbooks, lectures, worksheets, quizzes, and tests. You also follow a curriculum and the teacher's manual is what you use to assess your child. The traditional method is what most public and private schools use.

Popular curricula include:

Abeka

ACE/PACE

Alpha Omega Publications

BJU Press

Christian Liberty Press

Notgrass

Saxon Math

The Classical Method

This philosophy is very extensive. Basically, it is based upon three phases of learning: concrete (Kindergarten-5th grade), analytical (6th-8th grade), and abstract (high school). Language is a focal point of classical education and links all the subjects together. Learning is accomplished through words (writing and speaking) rather than photos, drawing, and video. Humanity is highly appreciated and is believed to possess a "divine spark." This form of education is derived from the methods of education used in Ancient Greece, Rome, Egypt, and Mesopotamia. It is also sometimes referred to as The Socratic Method.

Popular curricula include:

A Well-Trained Mind

BiblioPlan

Classical Academic Press

Classical Conversations

IEW

Memoria Press

Veritas Press

The Story of the World

Charlotte Mason

Founded on Christian beliefs, those who follow Charlotte Mason's philosophies believe that the Bible is the highest form of knowledge. Through the years, however, this philosophy has evolved to include secular beliefs, as well. A student of Charlotte Mason enjoys nature studies and living books. Read-alouds, journaling, handicrafts, and an appreciation for the arts are found in this method. The philosophy is based on educating the "whole child." This means that habits are formed, and students are directed toward good discipline. Atmosphere plays a huge role in how students learn as their world (and life) become their classroom.

Popular Curricula include:

Ambleside Online

Any living book

Apologia

Masterbooks

My Father's World

Simply Charlotte Mason

TruthQuest

Unschooling

Parents who align with the unschooling philosophy believe that all learning should be child-led. You, as the parent, are not the teacher. Parents are only there to guide and assist when needed. Children are naturally curious, and you only need to foster their natural desire to learn. For children, learning is a way of life.

This is also known as the Relaxed method. Every unschooler looks different because every child is different. With the unschooling philosophy, you will see a lot of self-research, exploration, and field trips.

Unit Study Method

Parents who follow the unit study method believe that a child should spend time focusing on one topic at a time. All subjects are woven into this theme, and instead of just skimming the surface, you dig deep. It is very hands-on and immersive.

Popular Curricula include:

Gather Round

Weaver

Notgrass

Eclectic Homeschooling

Many families will find that this category sums them up. Here, the philosophies tie many other (or all) philosophies together. You like a little Classical here and a little Charlotte Mason there. It's a "whatever works for you" style.

Now, this is not a complete list. There are others such as School at Home, the Montessori Method, the Waldorf Method, literature-based schooling, online schooling, and the Multiple Intelligence Method, to name just a few.

If you want, I want to encourage you to dig deeper into these philosophies and methods in order to discover what style works best for you and your family. The internet is full of information in these areas.

But I also want you to be aware that you can even make up your own philosophy. You can mix and match philosophies. Being a homeschool evaluator, I've seen more methods than you can imagine. There are the methods I mentioned above, but on top of that, I've seen everything from Funschooling to Outside Schooling, and from Travel Schooling to YouTube Schooling. As long as you can justify learning and whatever works for you works, this is your method. There's no judgement here.

I've spent many nights praying and thinking about each of my kid's personalities, strengths, and weaknesses. Along with my husband, I've carefully put together my own philosophy and method. It works for us. If I have this freedom, then so do you. Enjoy this process.

Chapter XIV

Some Thoughts on Standardized Testing

I decided to dedicate an entire chapter to the standardized test. Why? Because it is such a huge tool in evaluating students, yet it is such a debated topic among homeschool parents. I, of course, have my own personal opinions on the subject, and I think you might find them very useful.

Here's the truth. I actually administer tests to homeschoolers per parent request. I see different motivations for it. Some I agree with, and some I don't. But overall, I believe that a standardized test, if used properly, can be a very useful tool. First, let me explain how the test usually works.

When a student is tested, their knowledge is graded against a norm. This norm is the average score taken from a large group of students, of the same age or grade, from all over the United States or a particular area. That average score is usually marked at 50. If you are above the average, your score will be above 50, and if you are below the average, it will be under 50. It's much like a doctor's office, where your child's height and weight are scored on a percentile.

Here's another way of looking at it. Let's say you score 89 on a test. That score means that you scored higher than 89% of the other students who took that same test.

Some great examples of a norm-referenced test that you might encounter include the California Achievement Test, the Iowa Test of Basic Skills, the Stanford Achievement Test, and TerraNova. Even the ACT, SAT and IQ Test are considered "norm" tests.

The Worst Part of School

Sometimes in life you need to do things that you don't want to do in order to do the things that you do want to do. And in order to do the things you want to do well, many times we have to take tests. Passing a test can mean that you will be able to go to the school you need to go to in order for you to pursue the career of your dreams. This is nothing you don't already know.

But practice is important. Every person who will need to pass and score well on a test needs to practice taking tests. Taking tests is truly an art form. Many tests, rather than grading how smart you are, grade how well you trained for the test.

One reason to take a standardized test is to prepare a child so that you can provide every opportunity for them to pursue success. Practicing allows them to get comfortable with the stressful environment, allows them to understand how to take the test, and even teaches them how to focus.

In contrast, a standardized test should never be used as a tool to establish a ranking of how smart or dumb a student is, the degree to which a student succeeded or failed that year, or as a reflection of how valuable a person is.

For many, this is old news; we completely agree with all of this. Never should we rank our children or label them based on their test scores. But we are creatures of habit. When you were in school, you may have passed by the photos of valedictorians from years before and felt that tinge of envy. You may have fought to stay within the first 100 or 50 percent of the top of the class. You might have compared your grades and scores to your friends.

We did that, and we still do it all the time, at home, at work, and even with our kids and spouses. We want to be special. We want our kids to be special, to be better at something. It makes us feel good. But when we fail, we feel hopeless, discouraged, and sometimes overwhelmed.

You would be surprised at how many parents do this to themselves, the disappointed looks on their faces when their child scores below the 50 mark. I've heard parents confess, *It's my fault. We really slacked on math this year, and now I'm paying for it.* Or they'll even ask... *Does this mean I need to repeat a grade?* Or, *Do I have to send them back to school now?*

The focus becomes the score, the number, and not on what your child actually knows and who they are. A test score can never reflect who anyone truly is.

Sometimes, our child's lack of a high score is not because we didn't push them or work with them. Sometimes, it can be a red flag for learning disabilities. For our purposes, testing is a great opportunity to help a parent find alternative ways to teach and provide materials for their child.

I have often found myself asking questions of parents after testing their child, "Have they been diagnosed with a learning disability?" Or, I might ask specific questions about their reading experience, about math, and even about writing struggles. I've witnessed many light bulbs go off in parents' heads as they found that the test led them to a discovery of a learning disability. This, in and of itself, is utter relief.

Yes, it's a relief to many parents, when, after struggling and struggling with their child for months on a subject, they find out that it's not laziness, disobedience, or stupidity, but rather that your child could have dyslexia, dysgraphia, or even ADHD. Now a door has just swung open, a door that leads to a road with tried-and-true ways, traveled by professionals and parents who have experienced the same struggles that you have, a road that has been paved by those who have traveled it ahead of you, and now there's hope.

This is a possible result from standardized tests.

Another way to properly use a standardized test is to help properly place a child. It's a good guide. Many homeschool curricula use the guideline of a standardized test, but many do not. So, make sure to find out whether they have a placement test you can use for placing your child.

When your child has already been diagnosed with a learning disability, standardized tests can really help guide you to the right placement. These situations have always been the hardest to administer, especially if the parent is still in the mindset of ranking their child based on their scores. But, remembering to use the test as a way to find where your child will be successful, where they can thrive, will only help them. This is another correct way of using the results from a standardized test.

I'll admit, it's never easy to hear that our child is in a below-average percentile. I have a child like that. Developmentally, she is two years younger than her peers. It's a very hard pill to swallow, but I like to remind myself that, not only is this not a reflection of who she is, but this percentile ranking was non-existent not too long ago.

Remember our dear friend, Horace Mann? He's the one who introduced standardized testing to the public schools. The purpose was to provide "a single standard by which to judge and compare the output of each school" and to gather objective information about teaching quality.

That was it—the entire purpose. Not to rank children, but to rank how well schools and teachers were doing. But the truth is bigger even than that. Nothing about the Prussian model was focused toward the goal of educating unique individuals; they were instead focusing on forming a group of obedient factory workers who would be educated enough to work well, read well, and calculate well, but who wouldn't question leadership. Their objective was for all students to have similar experiences, and have a standardized ability to produce.

Reflecting on all of this, it's important to consider the different state and country homeschooling laws. Yes, some will require a standardized test. Some will not. It's always a good idea to become familiar with the homeschool laws that govern you where you live. But either way, make sure you understand how to handle the outcome.

Your children are watching you. If you respond poorly to their scores, this will be projected onto them. You might even make the decision to not even show them their score and keep it to yourself. But whatever you decide to do, it's really important to take the time to know how you will handle the results.

But we've talked a lot about academics, testing and curriculum, so let's discuss something more intimate, the *real* reason that so many of us parents want to homeschool: Making the most of these precious years.

CHAPTER XV

WHO IS YOUR CHILD'S FAMILY?

OHANA MEANS FAMILY, AND FAMILY MEANS NO ONE GETS
LEFT BEHIND.

STITCH

I want to take some time to define two very important words: *Family*
and *Community*.

These are not subjective words, as some might think, but terms that describe very specific roles we take on in our lives.

Let's start with family.

Regardless of whether your family functions well or is dysfunctional, a
family is a unit that is connected through marriage and parenting. This
includes parents, siblings, grandparents, uncles, aunts, cousins, nieces, and
nephews, whether through blood or adoption.

The immediate family consists of Mom and Dad and their children. When
the parents cannot take on the responsibility of their role, another member
of the family will become their guardian. When that cannot happen, adoption or fostering happens. Adoption is when a child officially becomes a
member of another family, outside of their original family. Fostering is not
a family, but rather, the community reaching out to help.

Now let's look at community.

A community is the outstretched arm that extends to the family. It is a family's support group and accountability partner that come alongside to help when a family needs support.

The community is a social unit. It is a group of people who share a common interest, a set of norms, nationality, ethnicity, set of customs, religion, values, and/or identity. They can connect through being (or gathering) in the same physical location, and also—thanks to technology, through social media and gaming. But the key here is that community members are not related through marriage or parenthood.

The True Role of the Family

I spent some time looking at documents (both secular and religious), and chatting with parents and educators alike to arrive at some of these conclusions. Surprisingly (but not really), the responses were very similar. So let me share my thoughts regarding the role of the family.

The family *should* provide a safe place for its members as they grow and mature.

To prepare for a future living outside the family, socialization first happens inside the family. Yes, I said socialization, as it is the family that takes a child on their first socialized "field trip" with others. Do you remember the first time your child was outside of the home with others? Someone in the family was probably there with them.

The family provides nurture, attachment and provides for the basic needs of a person. Each family member relies on the others for something, and they function as a unit. When one is injured, the others suffer.

Biblically speaking, parents have the primary role of responsibility. This includes what children are taught, whether that be how to load the dishwasher or where and how they are educated. Also where they live, what foods are available to eat, what activities they are involved with, etc... (Gal. 4:1-2, Prov. 1:7, Deut. 6:6-9).

This isn't just biblical, though. Even the state and federal governments recognize that the parent has the final say. I find this to be true in both the doctor's office and in the classroom. Unless a child is being harmed or neglected, the immediate parent or guardian is always right and has the final say.

I think it is very clear that our roles as parents are tremendous. We carry a huge responsibility, and we should not take this role lightly.

The Role of the Community

The community is there to help support a family when that family cannot function the way it was meant to.

Some examples include: fostering, churches, community farms and/or grocery stores, schools, hospitals, friends, support groups, and the list goes on. Community not only provides resources for parents (schools are an example), but also provides for spiritual and physical needs. Community is there to lift family members up when families cannot do so for themselves.

> COMMUNITY — MEANING FOR ME 'NURTURING HUMAN CONDITION' — IS OUR SURVIVAL. WE HUMANS WITHER OUTSIDE OF THE COMMUNITY. IT ISN'T A LUXURY, A NICE THING; COMMUNITY IS ESSENTIAL TO OUR WELL-BEING.
>
> FRANCES MOORE LAPPE

The bible is also clear on this matter. We are to commune with each other regularly, bearing one another's burdens, loving at all times, encouraging each one and coming together in unity (1 Cor 1:10, 1 Thess 5:14, Col 3:13, Gal 6:2, Prov. 27:17, Rom. 12:5).

> THE BIBLE KNOWS NOTHING OF SOLITARY RELIGION.
>
> JOHN WESLEY

A community is a necessary part of our human lives.

But, as with anything, humans tend to corrupt things, and we have corrupted the way things were meant to function. I believe that everyone can agree with this.

Now Education

In regard to education, the parent has the responsibility to choose how their child will be educated. In the past, physical and local communities consisted of people of the same mindset, the same worldview for most. So, naturally, sending your child to be educated by someone with the same views you have yourself was a good idea—and it still is, especially when you cannot perform that function yourself and you have similar goals.

But society grew; technology grew. Local and state governments became more assertive and took on more responsibilities. Churches and local communities became less involved. Schools changed, transformed, and became melting pots of ideas and teachings. Some would say that schools started to teach the agenda of the state. And in a sense, they did, because schools became state institutions.

When it comes to caring for individuals, schools also began to take on that role, though not at first, and not because they forced themselves into that role, but rather because parents, friends, local support groups, churches, and immediate communities freely gave this authority to them. Increasingly, this level of care came to be seen as a burden, and many would simply say, "Just let someone else do it. I mean, that's why we pay taxes, right?"

So now we have a society that, over time, has slowly given up their roles as parents to others without batting an eye. We don't question their agenda, we don't question how they're doing it, we just do it because that's what you do now. It's what my mom and dad did. It's what their parents did. So why not me? It's just easier.

The role of the school system has become a powerhouse. But for most, their morality, their teachings, do not align with the individual convictions of the family.

So, is it too late to get your authority back? The answer is yes, you can get it back. But it does take work and determination. We'll talk about this more later.

But let's say that you do agree with everything the traditional schools do. A lot of people do. And a lot of these parents still homeschool, but they homeschool for other reasons. One of those reasons might be that they see a lack of supervision, correction, and understanding.

Going back to when I first decided to homeschool, it was pretty normal to see special education teachers fall ill or need to take a day off or two. Some schools didn't even have a teacher explicitly designated as the special education teacher. Substitute teachers were hired, instead. Accordingly, their understanding of each child was not up to par. They often allowed kids to wander, take control of the classroom, and generally take advantage of the situation, all without the consent (or even knowledge) of the parent. In fact, parents were rarely consulted, if they were even consulted at all.

We could go on and on discussing different situations, different examples, but what it comes down to is this: many parents have freely, blindly, and submissively given up their role as parent to an institution that does not—and cannot—have their children's best interest at heart. They have been given a responsibility that they cannot handle. They are overrun, underpaid, and in many cases, teaching against the values that a family may hold dear.

I am aware, though, that this is not always the case. There are many local community schools that function beautifully, and I want to take a moment to give them a round of applause. But for many parents, especially if you are homeschooling or considering homeschooling, this is not the case.

Another thing to consider is this: When a parent freely allows the school to educate and care for their children, many things happen in that building that are not communicated to the parents. Teachers and staff assume that parents have given them full reign to teach whatever the state has asked, and rightly so.

For example, a school can bring in speakers, and assign books and classwork that go against the family's core beliefs. A school can discipline and have counseling sessions with students in ways that are never discussed and will never be discussed. In fact, many counselors have told parents that what has been said between them and their child is private and they don't have the right to know.

They have the authority to label your child as having one or more disabilities through tests, meetings, and observations. They then document this and share the information with teachers and students. This, as many of you know, opens the door for opinions and stereotypes to be formed.

And worst of all, many parents are never informed that this is going on or are in a position to see any of this happening.

Stacey's Struggle

One year, I had a middle school student, Stacey, who struggled. I had a lot of students with a lot of baggage, but this one in particular stood out to me. It started slowly. Stacey would make comments in class towards other students; ridiculous things, like, "You stink. Don't get near me," or, "You forgot your homework again? Surprise, surprise." She would comment on their hair, their clothes, basically anything, and then she would always end it in a laugh—a laugh that sent chills down your spine.

This went on for a while, and other teachers noticed it, too. It was talked about in faculty meetings, in lunch rooms, and even other students discussed this whenever she wasn't around. It was very sad.

Now, you would think that one of the first things we would do would be to contact the parents, and eventually we did. The parents were responsive and already aware of this situation, since she behaved this way at home and with her social group in the neighborhood. Because of that, Stacey was given counseling sessions and other outside interventions.

But the tide quickly shifted. Instead of insulting others, Stacey's insults became directed more toward herself. The kids already disliked her, so there was no sympathy there. She had already disrespected the teachers enough that they just ignored her or didn't care. Any outsider coming in would notice it right away; it really was devastating. The school environment that she was in was obviously dysfunctional. She needed to get out. It didn't matter at that point whether it was a private school, another public school, or even homeschooling. She just needed a fresh start, with interventions, of course, to help her transition.

But that wasn't an option. Not in her parent's eyes or even in the eyes of the school administration. Their position was, "We can fix this. We just need to try something else."

But the reality was that she was already hated and disliked by her peers, and even by her mentors. She had already been stereotyped, and word spreads quickly through a middle school. But the school had exhausted their resources. They were just trying new punishments, assigning new mentors, and retrying what they had already tried. But no one can heal in a hostile environment—and that was where Stacey was.

I spoke to her parents often. As far as anyone could see, her home environment was stable. There was no divorce, no loss of job, no neglect, no abuse. But there was one problem.

You see, her parents did care about her, and they had her best interests in mind, but they felt helpless. They continued to put blind faith in a system that wasn't working.

And, believing themselves to be incapable of helping their daughter, they just kept expecting the school's efforts to eventually work. As a result, they gave their authority over to the schools without even realizing what they had done.

Moving Stacey to a new school, or homeschooling her, was never considered. In fact, I specifically remember hearing a conversation at a meeting where the mom said, "I wish I could just take Stacey home and just school her there, but she's too far gone. Only the counselors, the teachers, and her medications can help her now."

This was so sad to see play out, and those parent-teacher conferences left me feeling just awful for everyone involved. I'll continue Stacey's story in a bit, but let's take a moment to think about this.

For many parents, when you mention that they could homeschool, their first response is, "I could never do that," or, "I'm not smart enough," or something along those lines.

Sometimes we forget that we live in a world that has abundant technology. We have access to social media, search engines, websites, online communities, physical communities. We have transportation, the internet, an endless supply of resources. There are free online curricula, professionals willing to chat for free, and experienced moms with tons of advice (sometimes, whether you want it or not). There is always someone with a phone number, an email address, a website that will point you in the right direction.

But sometimes we just don't do it; for two reasons, I believe.

1) We're overwhelmed and we can't find direction, so we give up or never get started.

2) We're insecure about our ability as parents to educate.

Sometimes, both.

We need a wakeup call. As parents, we have a responsibility to guide our children and make choices for our children regarding pretty much everything.

But it's not easy. On top of everything else, we also need perseverance, motivation, and determination in order to accomplish this—and I mean daily. This is a daily commitment.

A Spiritual Aside

I want to take a moment and come from a spiritual perspective, because that is my heart.

When summing up this chapter, I can't deny the existence of God and the influence of His hand on our lives as parents. He, Himself, established the family system. He designed the function and role of each member of the family. He required us to be involved in each other's lives as a community, like-minded, in unity, bearing one another's burdens.

This is His design.

But as humans, we're broken, and we easily give in to corruption and manipulate God's design. We are lied to, tricked, and even through traditions and culture, we believe false ideas without batting an eye.

When we become aware and strive to get back to the original design, which for most people coincides with secular beliefs (regarding the roles of family and community), we find that we have the authority to make strong and wise decisions about our child's education and training. But that also scares us to death.

And in a sense, it should. But the comfort lies in that we are not doing it alone. God's hand is guiding us and directing our footsteps. His eye is watching and His hand is working in our lives to help us do what He has called us to do.

We can rest assured that we are capable, because the One who created us made us capable.

And when it comes to being overwhelmed, sometimes, as we push through, we have to pray and trust that God will provide. And He will. There are too many stories to prove that He will.

As believers, we should remember that perseverance, motivation, and determination all come from God. It's not something that comes from within ourselves, but something that He Himself gives us as we draw closer to Him. So, as you go about your days, working, homeschooling, playing, praying, know that He has a plan for your kids' lives. He has made each child to be unique. You just have to get out of the way so that He can guide you (and them) through this journey.

Stacey's Struggle—Part 2

There's not much left of Stacey's journey to tell. To be honest, after she left for high school I never heard from her again. But I do know that for the three years she was with us, her depression, self-loathing, and bullying got steadily worse. It's just a sad story with loose ends that were never tied up. But she's not the only child who's had this experience. And hers is not the only family that's had to go down this well-paved road.

Now, all we have left to us is to glean from it whatever lessons we can. Are we like Stacey's parents? Are we stuck, just going with the flow out of fear, insecurity, or blind faith? If so, think about what you can do to change, and honestly, I implore you to write this down. There is so much power in writing things down.

Do We Get to Choose Our Community?

There's a phrase, "You get to choose your friends, but not your family." Have you heard it? It's great, isn't it? It means that the family has a say in who they commune with.

Remember, a community is a group of like-minded individuals. Why would you communicate with a group of people who didn't have the same standards you do?

So, if you don't agree with the school and the community within the schools, thank God that we can choose not to commune with them. That means you can choose your friends, your church, your synagogue, your homeschool co-op, the place where you volunteer, even where you work. You have that option.

Okay, maybe it's not that easy. But it is possible, and sometimes there must be sacrifices. Ask any homeschool family if they've had to sacrifice anything in order to surround themselves with like-minded people.

We all have a story. Some of our stories are more dramatic than others.

When I resigned from my job we lost an entire income, and at the time, I was the breadwinner. Our family was growing, the housing market had just crashed, and we were forced to downsize.

But the money issue was not my main struggle. I had built a name for myself as a teacher. I'd spent years climbing the teacher ladder. I was becoming a mentor and a role model, not only to my students but to other educators. I was convinced that no one could replace me. No one could do my job better than me.

Letting go of that was harder than letting go of the money—at least for me.

My husband also made some sacrifices at his job. More than he has ever told me, I'm sure. To put it lightly, it was a tough transition.

But we made that sacrifice because we knew we had a higher calling. So, we needed to adjust our lives to align with the original function of the family. Plus, by homeschooling, I got to see my boys all the time.

Even though our community didn't change very much, the function of (and reliance upon) our community did change. Sure, I lost my teacher friends, but in all honesty, I was never super close to them.

We were very active in our congregation, even before I resigned. My husband led Bible studies, and I was on the praise and worship team. But that really meant nothing when it came to our congregation's community. We didn't share burdens, call one another, or even hang out. Honestly, we were just too busy.

Now I'm busy with my kids, and I have to be proactive with building relationships within my congregational community. We assigned more value to taking on leadership roles at our congregation than we did before.

We also realized that we needed to connect with other homeschooling families. We felt the need to seek out families that were like minded, with similar goals and a common purpose, people who would be easy to connect with because they understood what we were going through. We visited homeschool co-ops, joined some, and basically, we decided who we would hang out with. We also, by default, decided who our kids hung out with.

Then, of course, there came the idea of curriculum and homeschool materials. We decided what books our children would read, what curriculum would be used, and when to use it. And when we have to outsource, we decide who gets to take on that role, and we found plenty of resources to choose from.

Sure, there is the potential that you'll find yourself living in a bubble. But the best part is, you get to decide what kind of bubble and how big your bubble will be. Or, you may not have a bubble. That's entirely your call. That is the freedom you have as a homeschooling family. You get to make these choices freely.

So now I want to pose a question to you. The question is, if you're not homeschooling now, are you willing to make that sacrifice?

And if you are homeschooling and you have been for some time now, reflect on the sacrifices you've made. Were they worth it?

If you have a journal, write these things down now and spend some time reflecting on them and how far you've come.

Letting It Go

We have now established the role of the family, the role of the parents, and the role of the community. And now that we know we have choices, let's go a little deeper.

Ask yourself this question.

When you decided to homeschool, did you fully take on your role as a parent, or did you still hang onto your former ideas, benchmarks, and standards?

As an evaluator, I see this a lot.

Parents who were formerly educated by the public school system, or even in private schools (who actually have similar agendas, but with a twist), bring their baggage to their homeschooling world.

Hear me out, here. I'll explain.

Many parents start to homeschool, yet mimic the public school in their homes. They use a similar curriculum, follow the same academic schedule, test their kids on a regular basis, etc... and for some, that's absolutely fine. That's what you want. You've studied, thought things through, and you want to mimic public school because you think it's the best method for your children. You've decided that you agree with their teachings, their academic standards, and schedules, and that's great.

But many families don't operate that way, and when they don't operate that way, which is normal, they become frightened or insecure. Or they might respond by changing their homeschool environment into a school-like environment, which in turn may cause a ton of stress.

I once evaluated a family who was going through a crisis. The father was a foreign national married to an American. He lived with his family in America, but he needed to fix some things to make his citizenship fully compliant. One thing he had to do was go back to his original country, and he decided to take his children.

School books were packed, and all was well. They made it to his home country, their extended family welcomed them into their homes with open arms, but there was one big problem: now that they were in the father's home country, they found that they would not leave. To make a long story short, they were all stuck in their father's native country for six months. And even though the daughters were American citizens, they weren't allowed to leave, either.

Needless to say, between the hardships of having to stay in that country and the lack of schooling materials, the girls had to take some time off from school.

At the homeschool evaluation, the parents were in tears, absolutely terrified that they had ruined their daughters' academic career, that the school districts and everyone would disapprove of their hardship. They were heartbroken and concerned that I was going to require them to put them back in public school.

To their surprise, that didn't happen. I let them know that a family crisis can lead to important and valuable lessons in life that no school book could teach them. They learned about the importance of family, how to handle difficult situations properly and patiently. What they missed from schooling they could certainly make up.

Why do we tie ourselves to a schedule that doesn't fit our family or our lives? But it happens all the time. We feel guilty when life happens, but we forget the important, teachable moments that occur when life happens.

Wanting More

Not every homeschooling year faces a crisis like that one. Sometimes, it's just an illness or an injury that needs some recovery time. So, your schedule may not be affected to that extent.

When you thought of the question I posed earlier: *When you decided to homeschool, did you fully take on your role as a parent?* You may have fallen into the pit of frustration, fear, or insecurity that many homeschooling parents can feel. You may have seen those traditional schooling techniques sneak their way into your day-to-day life.

And you didn't like it.

You sense that you want more. Or maybe you find yourself saying, "This is not how I planned to raise my kids."

First, let me say that this is why so many experienced homeschooling parents suggest that the first thing you should do when you start homeschooling is write out the reasons you made the decision.

Why are you deciding to homeschool? Talk with your spouse. Make sure you are on the same page and then write the reasons down.

Write as many as you possibly can, but then try to narrow it down to one or two. Once you're done, put it in a spot where you can see it easily and refer to it whenever you need to recall why this became something worth sacrificing for in the first place.

Keeping your reasons in perspective while shopping for curriculum, picking out co-ops, and even planning field trips can really help you keep your focus. And, most importantly, revisit and reevaluate your "reasons" and "goals" yearly.

It's always natural to want more for your child than what the traditional school system has laid out. We have that parental instinct, and we know that, deep down inside, we have a role to play in our children's education.

Thankfully, every child is different; they weren't meant to be forced into a cookie-cutter life. You, the parent, have that freedom to keep your children away from that.

The uniqueness of each family is what makes all of life so unique. Yet, the unity and like-mindedness between family members and their communities needs to be cultivated. Every family has their own set of moral standards, and like I said before, the traditional school system does not always align with these convictions. The parent and family-chosen community must step up to the plate.

I'll address that more in the upcoming chapter, but first, I want to address learning disabilities and special needs.

Sometimes, parents will pull their kids out of school and chose homeschool because they see that public schools are not caring for them or recognizing them the way they should.

So, let's look at that.

CHAPTER XVI

LEARNING DISABILITIES AND SPECIAL EDUCATION

Carlos

Carlos was always in trouble at school. As the teacher taught, he would walk around, tap his pencil, click his pen, throw away yet another sheet of paper, or make random off-topic comments to his friends. Plus, in the few instances when he was actually sitting, he couldn't sit still. Any and every possible position a child could sit in, Carlos would demonstrate it several times throughout any given day.

He drove everyone crazy. The teacher lost valuable class time trying to redirect him, clean up after him, and even wait for his "moments" to end.

Carlos had ADHD. Everyone knew it. The school met with his parents, filed all the paperwork perfectly, and everything looked like it would be taken care of. But, of course, it wasn't.

In time, Carlos' teacher gave up on him. She ignored him, stopped redirecting him, and continued to just let him do whatever he wanted to do. She had so much more to deal with: twenty-seven other students, to be exact.

Carlos' grades dropped, and his attention span shortened ever more until he just didn't care. He disrespected adults and peers alike. He became a force to be reckoned with. Mom and Dad were furious, and they had to make a choice.

They could either continue down this path, or they could try something new.

They decided to homeschool.

If you knew how many times the exact events in the above example happened, it would surprise (or maybe it might not). Given the number of instances of such things as ADHD, autism , dyslexia, or even giftedness very few children actually fit the profile of the "normal" child. And all of these children need more assistance, direction, grace, patience, and time.

To their credit, the public schools do try to accommodate. They have a protocol. They have specific teachers designated to assist with learning, they conduct meetings with parents and staff, they devise response plans, allocate extra funding, and much more. But surprisingly enough, students still fall behind, or just simply get into trouble.

About the Protocol

Sometimes when the protocol is enacted, the teachers (and parents) are tempted to treat the student like a subject rather than a person. They put their hope in a system, allowing the program or algorithm to dictate what the next step should be, treating the student like a robot. This happens quite frequently.

I'll admit this, though. Sometimes, the protocol provides a good reference point, a springboard, so to speak. It's good for guidance. But the problem is that it's rooted in state laws and legalism. The protocol exists primarily to prove that the teacher did everything they could to help, providing a defense if something goes wrong.

Now, in defense of the teachers, we have some amazing special education and classroom teachers. They do care and they pour their hearts and souls into teaching. But with the pressure, the workload, the paperwork, and endless job requirements they have, kids with special needs and learning disabilities get brushed aside, and most of the time, it's not on purpose. It just happens.

A teacher can only do so much. And some do admit it. Remember, they're taking on the role of several parents. I've heard many stories about teachers who have asked parents to look into home education because they would get the accommodations they need that way. It's nothing shocking or new. Kids with learning disabilities and/or special needs need more than what the public school system has to offer.

In some cases, it's pride that keeps a child enclosed in a special education program. "We can fix this," is the attitude. Some feel that the college degree, the job title, their experience, and load of in-service classes makes them more qualified than the parent, and many teachers are not hesitant to remind you. Others are humble and not afraid to admit that they're wrong. But either way, the, "We know more than parents" attitude can push the parent into submission so parents can't do their jobs.

Now, in a healthy environment, parents and teachers work together to help the child, each acknowledging the other's job and role. This does happen, and when it does, the outcome may be very good for the child. The world needs more good special education teachers.

But most often, things gets complicated, and every teacher, parent and student has a unique story to tell. Schools rarely offer that healthy environment, and finding a good balance is sometimes better found outside of the public school system.

What it comes down to is fulfilling your role, and striking the right balance between those feeding into the lives of the child.

How We Thrive

Now, as many of you already know, my youngest daughter has Down Syndrome. Right away, we decided to homeschool her. Instead of using the school's special services, our insurance has paid for her physical, speech, and occupational services. Here are some things that make these services different from school services.

Independent services last year-round. There are no slow-downs at the beginning or end of the school year. There are no adjustment periods for a new teacher every year. As a homeschooling special needs parent, the only thing that slows you down is insurance. And usually, once that's under control, things go smoothly.

In homeschooling special needs children, paperwork is cut in half—probably more than half. It seems like 70% of a special education teacher's job is paperwork and meetings. They have so little energy and time left for their students that it's ridiculous. In fact, they'll hire a teacher's aide, just so they can get their work completed. In the homeschool environment, when you work with an independent therapist or tutor, the paperwork load diminishes. That means they have more time and energy to focus on your child and what they need.

Not only do you get one-on-one, uninterrupted, personal attention, but you can observe and be a part of your child's development. My daughter's therapist is very proactive about filling me in on every detail if I'm unable to observe. The schools don't ever offer this.

And most importantly, in my opinion, I get to choose who her therapist is.

Now, of course, not every learning disability or special needs situation qualifies for this kind of coverage. And if that is your case, what do you do?

Well, the first good news is that you have options. You can pay for services, or you can do your own due diligence research and find techniques and tips to help you. Both of these options are difficult and can take a lot out of you.

ADHD is extremely common. Dyslexia and other learning disabilities are, too. But believe it or not, there are a ton of resources out there. There are books and curricula that specifically cater to those issues. And beyond that, there are moms willing to listen and share advice, support, and encouragement.

One place you can go is my website where I've compiled a list that will give you resources and curriculum suggestions. It's a starting point.

But talking to other homeschool parents within your community is key. Why? Because, when social media and the internet don't give you the truth, they will. But not only that, they're a huge walking library of experience and wisdom that you can learn from.

As a mom with kids who struggle with learning disabilities and special needs, we face difficulties that many parents can't even imagine. Beyond the education and basic skills, there's the gossip, the behind-the-back whispers, the judgment, being left out, and things that make your life already difficult life, are made just a little more painful.

Understanding our God-given role is the first step. You are capable of succeeding as a parent. If you couldn't handle it, you would never have been given this job in the first place.

You'll put in hours and sweat. You'll endure emotional, and maybe even physical, pain. You'll have to get back on your feet, repeat yourself a million times, and then do it all again. No one understands what you do in your home when the doors are closed. But then again, no one understands your child like you do.

And your child needs you. You are their voice, their advocate. You are their comfort when they realize that they are not like other children. You are their encouragement, their cheerleader. They know that no matter what is said or what happens, you have their back.

Why wouldn't it be you who can educate them the best? No one can show them patience. Even when you think you've run out, when you slip up, when you yell or walk away in frustration, you always come back ready to try again.

They know you're there and that you'll always be there as long as you can.

Sometimes it's hard to find the motivation you need to keep going. Because this is hard. You get burned out. This is where you need to take some time to find your motivation. Do you look forward to cooking with them? Do you get excited when they read a word, or is it the time you spend cuddling on the couch watching a good movie? Find times that make you happy, keep finding moments together and hang onto those. Remember them when you want to give up.

Also remember to find free days, days that you can just take off and be—alone or together. Find family time, time with just you and your spouse, and even time alone, time to rejuvenate and collect yourself.

Find a support group that you can laugh and joke with, but also supports each other through tough times.

Each season with a special needs child is different and calls for different hats and different tools. But you'll always be their parent. Some seasons will be harder and will take more from you, but that doesn't always last. Some seasons will require you to stand back and observe. Either way, try to always find the good. Always try to find joy in the little silly things in life, as long as they're appropriate. But find joy. Find the positive in everything.

CHAPTER XVII

THE NEED FOR COMMUNITY

"TEACHING KIDS HOW TO FEED THEMSELVES AND HOW TO LIVE IN A COMMUNITY RESPONSIBLY IS THE CENTER OF AN EDUCATION."

ALICE WATERS

Kendall and her husband already had five beautiful children at the early age of twenty-seven. She always felt like she was pregnant—or at least nursing. It was her way of life. Maybe some of you can relate?

I met Kendall through a friend who was throwing a party for one of their kids.

Kendall and I hit it off great. We both had similar interests, likes, dislikes, and a handful of kids that were the same age.

"You know it's really hard," she said. "We don't get out much and my kids don't get to hang out with many kids their own age."

Me, being the extrovert that I am, I said, "Oh my goodness, we should hang out, for sure. Playdates, parks, you could even come out to our congregation. You would really love it."

We both agreed that it would be great to do that, but she didn't want to leave her home very much. In fact, she confessed to me later that she was

119

very uncomfortable being at the party but her husband had really wanted to get out and do something with some friends.

Part of her discomfort came from having a son on the spectrum. He was very difficult to handle at times, and quite frankly, she was embarrassed. She told me stories about being out grocery shopping and people making comments about how she needed to control her son better.

"He looks absolutely normal. No one would know that he has autism unless they spoke to him. I think that's why people are less understanding in public. But sometimes, it's just easier to stay at home," Kendall said.

I did go to her home a few times. The kids played and we spent so much time chatting. She was an absolute delight. However, I think I was one of her only friends outside of her family.

I would invite her to places, to our homeschool co-op, to our congregation (which was literally down the street). She did come a few times, but never once did she feel comfortable. She was a true introvert. Being an introvert isn't a bad thing, but when one's introverted nature causes their family to suffer, then it can be a problem. She would tell me over and over how she just wished that she could make friends. She knew that her kids were suffering because of it.

Her oldest was an extrovert. He was always wanting to go out and play with his neighborhood friends, and to play video games online with others or begging Kendall to just take him somewhere. In fact, many times when we left, tears were shed. Not just by him, but by other kids. They always had a hard time saying goodbye.

This was her struggle, and regardless of how hard it was for her to be out in public she knew that things needed to change. Regardless of how difficult it was to get the kids dressed, their lunches packed, and out the door on time, she knew what she needed to do and talked to me about it a lot.

The Beauty of Community

Most families recognize the beauty of community. A community is our support group, our outstretched arm, the people we go to for encouragement, honesty, and advice, and vice-versa. We share trials, sadness, and joy. We mourn and celebrate together. It's what holds us up and keeps us going. It keeps us humble, balanced, and holds us accountable. When one family is down, the community rallies around them to get them back on their feet.

There are so many different types of communities: neighborhoods, sports organizations, sewing groups, vegan groups, scouting groups, churches, synagogues, and of course, homeschool groups. You can connect in different ways, through meet-ups, phone calls, work, and social media. Everyone can find a community to join if they just keep looking.

Co-opping

Homeschool Co-oping is very popular with many families, allowing groups of families to share the responsibility of teaching each other's children. But each co-op looks different.

Some co-ops charge per class, kind of a la carte. The teachers are hired and paid and will track grades and homework throughout the year. Usually, children are dropped off at the co-op location and picked up after the classes are over.

Some co-ops are parent-led. Parents teach a class and assume responsibilities throughout the day, cleaning, bringing food, selecting which classes will be offered, even organizing the meet-up places.

Some are once-a-week playdates.

Some consist of a handful of families meeting up to do science labs and messy experiments.

Some are intensive and specific to a particular curriculum. Classical Conversations and Tapestry of Grace are two examples.

Some co-ops are exclusive, with entry granted pending an interview. Some are religion-based, some are secular, and costs range all the way from free to very expensive. Co-ops could meet once a week, twice a week, or even five days a week.

Co-opping is so unique. It's a way to build community, socialize, and learn.

Don't Leave Them At Home

Co-opping is not for everyone, but it is very important. Even if you chose as a family not to use a co-op, it is something you should consider doing at least once in your homeschool journey.

A friend of mine, Katie, who happens to be a second-generation homeschooler, once said to me, "It's a good idea to have your kids taught by someone else for at least a year, and before they graduate. The homeschools I've seen where children were taught only by their parents have a much harder time, whether they go to college, technical school, or even just a job. Getting used to someone who isn't going to account for weak excuses or someone with a different teaching style is important for learning how to deal with real life." (10)

A co-op can fill that need when you bring your son or daughter to an environment with like-minded people because, unlike public school, you can choose who gets to teach your kids and for how long. This helps your kids to see what real life looks like. Parents share the responsibilities of teaching, even correcting bad behavior; students take on roles such as cleaning, assisting parents, and more. They get to know one another, socialize, and community is nurtured.

Okay, so I know that not every parent is perfect. But I can say, first hand, that I've had some crazy parents discipline my children in ways I disagreed with. Not anything abusive, but things were not always handled the way I wanted them to be. I've also seen teachers handle assignments in ways I would disagree with, too.

We all can't be in total control of what happens in their lives all the time, but we can establish boundaries and qualifications. Some people want only certified teachers to teach their kids, while some want only Christian parents to teach.

When something goes off-track, though, or just different, it's so good for your kids to learn how to adjust to it. It's real life.

More Benefits of Co-ops

Getting together with other homeschool families is just good for your soul. It makes you feel like you're not alone in the world. You can learn from each other, share curriculum, tips, and encouragement. Most of the good stuff I know now, I learned from other homeschool moms.

It takes a lot of the pressure off of you. I can't teach Spanish to my kids to save my life, but someone else can. Some people outsource math or science. Many parents just don't want to deal with dissections and messy things, but they can grade essays all day long. This is only possible through co-opping.

Within a co-op, your kids will find their closest friends. They'll get to learn with them. They can tell stories about the time they threw a pencil in the air and their friend caught it without even seeing it. Or, maybe the time they dissected a cow liver and they broke open the gallbladder and watched it ruin their friend's shoes (true story). They enjoy inside jokes, boys laugh at fart jokes, and girls do each other's nails during lunch. This is all possible with co-ops.

It's not for everyone, but it is something to consider.

Bundles and Sticks

I want to end this chapter with a summary of a familiar story: "The Bundle of Sticks." Aesop's Fables aren't just for kids, but adults, too, and this story really sums up why we need community—and most importantly, why we must come together in unity as a community.

A certain father had three sons that argued quite often, so he sent them out to gather sticks. When they came back, each son had a bundle of sticks. The father then asked his sons to break their bundle. Each son tried and tried, but not one of them could break it.

Then the father untied the bundles and gave each son one stick. He then told them to break the single stick. each was able to break their stick with ease. The father said, "My sons, do you see how certain it is that if you agree with each other and help each other, it will be impossible for any enemy to injure you? But, if you are divided amongst yourselves, you will be no stronger than a single stick in that bundle."

There is strength in unity.

This story doesn't just apply to your family, but to communities, as well. We aren't created to be alone, but to work together and to be together. There are lots of places where you can find community. Homeschool co-ops are one great opportunity.

Now let's change gears a bit and chat about some other practical ways, besides co-opping, that can help you make the most of your years.

CHAPTER XVIII

PRACTICAL HOMESCHOOLING

I'm sure you've been here before. You're standing in line at the store waiting to pay for you groceries and your child is grabbing at the magazines, the sodas, or candy.

"Mom, just this once—please?!"

"No, not right now."

As the boredom continues, they either find something else they want you to buy or they start swinging from the cart or shelves.

"Stop. Please, stop." And then you redirect them.

You know people are watching and judging you as a parent. Your patience is tried as beads of sweat form on your brow.

Sometimes a stranger will say something. Not usually, but it happens. And there's a lot they can say. But there's one line that always gets on my nerves in a convicting and annoying kind of way.

"Enjoy them while they're young. It goes by fast."

You may have experienced this differently. Maybe it was at the park or at church. Maybe it was at a drive-through or the doctor's office. But I'm sure you've heard it said to you.

Here's the thing: that line is true.

Take these annoying words of wisdom to heart.

Are you enjoying your kids?

Sometimes, just enjoying them more and controlling them less is what it takes to really raise and teach a child.

Listening More

I once sat in on a teaching. It was about discipline, but I think it applies here, too. The teacher spoke about how his relationship with his son was "off." They never chatted or spoke, so one day he decided to spend some time finding out what his son enjoyed.

It was video games. His son was known to spend hours at a time on video games. Of all things, this annoyed his parents, but it was hardly surprising.

Dad went into his son's room, sat next to his son and started asking questions. As they talked, the dad listened intently, keeping his mouth shut. In the end, the dad decided to find a character trait or skill that he saw in his son while he spoke and shared his passion for video games—something strong and important. Then he said, "You know, I never realized how good you were at solving puzzles. And you're so focused."

He left it at that. He didn't add "But..." or, "I wish you would do this with that skill." Nope. He just enjoyed the best qualities of his son and focused on them.

We are out to help our children become the best they can possibly be, right?

And sometimes, the only way to do that is by allowing them to show us what that is. This requires us to take a back seat momentarily and listen to them. Pray, listen, observe, repeat. Try different things, go on different journeys, new field trips, hang out with new people, learn new skills, and so on. Some they will hate; some they will love, but give it time.

One of my close friends has a son who loves robotic competitions. She would have never known this if she hadn't taken him to a co-op. Another family I know has a child who loves writing poetry. She learned this from her grandmother and now their child enters poetry competitions.

Another friend of mine, Sally, has a daughter who is fascinated with gardening. The mom hates gardening and would have never discovered that her daughter loves it had she not purposely done a unit on botany with her.

When Sally started the Botany unit, she despised it. It was too much drawing and writing and plants... how boring. But she gave it a few weeks instead of giving up.

Around the third week she was outside on her own, drawing trees and plants in her own private journal. One of her projects was to start a butterfly garden. This was the pivotal point in her education. She was hooked. Now she has an entire garden with vegetables, berry bushes, and flowers that she maintains throughout the year.

Provide the things that spark your child's interests. Exposing them to different topics, skills, environments, and talents. Homeschool co-ops provide this easily, like I mentioned above, but grandparents, neighbor kids, congregations, and community events can do the same.

It's also about persistence. Sometimes you have to push them or force them to try something new. As parents, we know when to stop. Trust your instincts.

This is mostly about listening with open ears and eyes.

Right now, as I type, my son has been expressing an interest in starting his own business. So, we're working on a business plan for him and how we are to going to give him a "loan" in order to buy supplies. He is essentially learning economics (and how to wash the car.)

But to get there I had to listen to him. I had to ask questions.

Playing More

Twice a week, we spend the entire morning (and sometimes afternoons) taking my youngest daughter to therapy sessions.

On these mornings, I pack up the van with pencils, books, curriculum, and lunch. At first I was convinced we could get it all done, including the heavy stuff like writing and math.

Have you ever sat in a car with three kids for three hours? It just doesn't go well. Let's be honest.

After the first long "therapy day" I knew I had to adjust. Let me paint the picture.

The kids would have all their work setup but all they really wanted to do was go outside. I said, "No, we've got work to do." So I pulled out their work, opened the trunk of the van to make a little sitting area and let them get to work. There was bumping, pencil stealing, arguing, throwing, yelling, rolling around, you name it.

After three hours of this... I just couldn't do it, so I let them outside and said the heck with it, we'll do school at home and reevaluate.

The Next Day

The following day, I brought all their school work, but I focused on reading books and audio books. This worked for a while, but for three hours in the car? No way. So, after an hour of book reading and listening, we eventually spent the rest of the day outside.

It took a while to figure out what was going to work for these therapy-session days. I felt I had no choice but to call a family meeting. I addressed the struggle, and we briefly discussed what we could do to make sure their school work got done.

Here was the verdict: My kids needed to play outside.

There were three places where my daughter did therapy.

At speech therapy, "outside" was not an option. So, when we went there they did independent book work and/or audio books. They would be expected to sit in the trunk or their car seat and work diligently or there would be things taken away.

The second place we went to (physical therapy) was in a residential neighborhood. It had a sidewalk with no busy roads around. We could walk around or sit and read books together.

The last (and most visited) place had a large field behind it with seasonal ponds, trees, bugs, flowers, hills, ants, sticks—NATURE!—and a world the kids were dying to explore. There was no playground, no swing, just land and a lot of it. When we were there we would do more read-alouds and just play.

I would have to adjust their school work, possibly find different curricula, or more topical group studies, and allow for more independent work and exploration.

Here's what eventually happened.

On therapy day, I started to look forward to going. I would pack the bag full of books and maybe their grammar and writing journals. I started approaching science differently, more animal and nature topics: botany, insects, birds, etc. Lunch would be packed and off we'd go.

On our arrival, I would first let them play for the first hour and sometimes I would join in. There were days that they dug holes and built little bridges out of sticks. Sometimes, they would just dig. Many times this turned into an ant exploration, discovering how an ant hill works. Also exploring how ants bit.

Once they found a thick vine to swing on. They would swing over different lands and valleys. Sometimes that would become a portal to a different worlds. I was invited many times (actually I begged) to join in. But, unfortunately, my weight broke the vine and, as my son said, "You broke the portal!"

They found tadpoles and baby mosquitos. We once looked and tried to classify all the flowers we found with a field guide I borrowed from the library. We picked flowers and dissected them, and (using science terms) discussed how seeds were made. We've rolled down hills, raced across fields, and snuggled up and answered questions about life.

They once made a campfire circle. They placed large rocks for seats and more rocks surrounding the piles of sticks. We've read The Lord of the Rings there, Bible devotionals, books about botany, anything we were working through educationally at that season. But we did it together.

Our walks to and fro were filled with conversations and questions, hugs and laughter, running and rolling. These are memories that will stick and continue to bond us together for life. School time becomes quality time— much better than sitting in a car for three hours twice a week.

Now, sitting in the car still happens, just not for the full three hours. The car is where we do audio books, devotionals, read-alouds, and sometimes grammar, math, and writing independently. But as soon as they get antsy, I put it aside and default to something new.

Reading Together More

"THERE ARE FEW STRONGER FAMILY BONDS THAN THIS HABIT OF DEVOTING AN OCCASIONAL HOUR TO READING ALOUD, ON WINTER EVENINGS AT ANY RATE. THE PRACTICE IS PLEASANT AT THE TIME, AND PLEASANT IN THE RETROSPECT, IT GIVES OCCASION FOR MUCH BRIGHT TALK, MERRY AND WISE, AND QUICKENS FAMILY AFFECTION BY MEANS OF INTELLECTUAL SYMPATHY. INDEED, THE WONDER IS THAT ANY FAMILY SHOULD NEGLECT SUCH A SIMPLE MEANS OF PURE ENJOYMENT, AND OF MORAL, AS WELL AS INTELLECTUAL CULTURE."

CHARLOTTE MASON

This is one activity that touches on almost everything. You can read about science, history, imaginary worlds, learn phonics, spelling, grammar just from observation. You can talk about your faith, build character, and bond more as family just by using the time you have been given as you read.

Just the simple act of curling up on the coach, laying out on the grass, or sitting in a tree and reading together makes memories that can never be replaced.

Plus, it slows you down. Think about it: sitting and reading makes you take time and enjoy each word on each page. You pay special attention to imagining the details of every character, location, animal, anything mentioned in the book. If it's non-fiction, no difference. Instead of video games, television, and tablets, where the images are given to you all at once, reading makes you draw from your own experiences to create new images in your mind, one at a time.

Now, reading aloud does lead to children building a love for books so that they are inspired to read on their own. And it encourages older kids to keep reading for enjoyment.

"THE MOST COMMON AND THE MONSTROUS DEFECT IN THE EDUCATION OF THE DAY IS THAT CHILDREN FAIL TO ACQUIRE THE HABIT OF READING."

CHARLOTTE MASON

Reading in general is a wonderful pastime—better than video games and television. It fills their minds with living ideas—ideas that they can build upon and explore at a deeper level. It inspires imagination and innovation. The smartest people in the world read weekly and are constantly desiring to learn more.

Reading builds character and empathy. It helps us see the choices people make and we learn from them. Whether they are successful or they fail, whether they are good or bad, we learn from all of them. We can also learn about different people and perspectives by learning and journeying with them through their stories, getting to know and understand people we would never meet in real life. Books are timeless that way.

No other discipline can do this.

Gaming More

I'm not talking about letting kids play video games all day long. When I say gaming more, I'm talking about physical games, guessing games, educational games, board games, and playground games that you play together as a family.

We all can see how Scrabble strengthens spelling, Clue gives us deductive reasoning, Monopoly teaches us about money—those are obvious. But there's so much more. In fact, there are actually games created to teach schooling concepts. There is also an entire philosophy out there where games are the primary method of teaching: Gameschooling.

I know a family who gameschools. Their walls are covered with shelves filled with games galore. Their children are a wealth of knowledge and creativity, and they know how to solve problems.

One of the qualities I've noticed about one of the boys is that he knew how to create little short-term goals. And because he had set the goals himself, he had the motivation to complete it. He had the confidence to delve into his abilities to do what he set his mind out to do.

Now, not all of us want to exclusively gameschool, but we do have access to their wonderful resources and we can use them in our homeschool. And there's a lot.

There are so many benefits to what these games have to offer apart from pure educational value. Of course, learning through play and a stress-free, anxiety-free, judgement-free environment is plenty to encourage any family to explore these options, but beyond that, the memories and bonding are immeasurable.

Do you have a memory from your childhood, something you did with your family that you'll never forget? Do you find yourself finding a special place in your heart for that thing?

Hobby More

One thing that we like to do as a family is play and build with LEGO® bricks. This started way back, before my sons could even say "LEGO."

I was teaching LEGO® engineering at homeschool co-op. Not by myself, you see; it was something my dad got me into. When he found out that I was teaching homeschoolers, he, being a retired engineer and former robotics coach, was so ready to dive into LEGO® robotics with his daughter.

He bought the first set and built and programmed a few bots. Then an expansion set was bought, and here we were, ready to teach several groups of homeschooled middle schoolers how to build their own. It was fun. It was like being schooled by my Dad all over again.

My boys watched me from a distance and started to come into my class to observe. Then we bought them a few LEGO® sets. We had a LEGO® birthday for one of them, and then my husband sat down one day and discovered just how relaxing this pastime was.

My husband was slightly addicted. What started as one set became two. Two simple sets became many larger sets. Eventually, the large sets became hauls of LEGO® bricks, and when I say hauls, I am not joking.

Next, he started buying and selling LEGO® bricks. He would bring home a set, sit with the boys, put it together, then decide whether he wanted to sell it or keep it.

The boys built LEGO® cities in their playroom that kept growing and growing. One of my boys wrote an entire constitution and even set up a government system for his LEGO® country.

Eventually the boys did take my Robotics/STEM LEGO® class at the co-op and they excelled. They worked with others on creating structures, coming up with plans, and even designing inventions.

Besides all of the educational value these little toys bring, it has also brought in a lot of character-building.

Just tonight, we are working on a 4,000-piece LEGO® model. Each of us, without arguing or fighting over pieces, assumed a role as either organizer, piece finder, or builder. My daughter wanted to build as well so she would skip ahead in the instructions to find the cool pieces on a separate iPad.

We worked together as a team. Nothing distracted us. We were focused and worked as one unit. These are skills that will only help them as they get older.

During this time there was no talking. In fact, we decided to listen to an audiobook while we worked.

What's so cool about having something special that your family does and learn together, is that it makes you unique. Plus, it's something that could be passed on to their kids.

What started as something my dad and I did together was turned into a family quality time. That's how it always is.

So with that thought—and as a side note—be careful with what you do with your kids. Those memories make an impact, and they stick. Make sure it's something that teaches character, values, respect, and love.

It can be anything from walking on the beach together to writing music together. It could be as simple as reading or fishing or as complex as starting a car washing business together or building furniture. Whatever you love to do, you can instill that into your children, plus all the other wonderful qualities that go along with it.

Remember who you are in their lives and take every moment to make that moment special, unique, enjoyable, and teachable.

Chapter XIX

Finding Your Identity

WITHOUT WORK, ALL LIFE GOES ROTTEN. BUT WHEN WORK IS
SOULLESS, LIFE STIFLES AND DIES.

ALBERT CAMUS

You are a leader, a teacher, a mentor, a parent. You are who God made you
to be. Unique, diverse, trendy, or not, you are you. No one can parent and
raise your kids the way you can.

But many times we get lost in all of this. We lose ourselves, our purpose,
and our goals.

Of course, it's always great to see how others do things to get ideas, watching others homeschool, asking questions, watching videos, listening to podcasts, those sorts of things. We know that more experienced parents can give us tips and a different perspective on things. But don't allow who you are to get forgotten in all of that. Don't forget your focus.

Ask yourself: Who am I doing all of this for? Is it for others to see, for others to admire? Is it for your pride, to prove to yourself that you're better than others? That your kids are scoring higher and getting the better jobs?

Do you aim to be the best at everything?

What kinds of expectations are you putting on yourself? Do you really think you can handle everything on five hours of sleep, coffee, and a protein shake without making mistakes? Do you expect to be flawless?

Do you realize that it's okay to make mistakes?

Do you expect yourself to do it all? It's okay to take a backseat sometimes. It's okay to let others help you. Did you know that it's a blessing to let someone help you?

Social Circles

Let's consider our social circles. Over the decades, the size of one's social circle has grown. The number of opportunists we're likely to have around us has grown.

Your social circle includes you, your family, and extends to your community. Your community could include your circle of friends at co-op, church, baseball, dance class, music lessons, mom or dad's groups. Then, within each little community there are different people with different lives.

You also have influencers that you listen to and watch, like political commentaries, Instagram feeds, YouTube channels, Facebook profiles, podcasts you're subscribed to, the list goes on.

That's a lot of people doing a lot of different things—and we only see a tiny portion. With your local community, you may see more struggles, but with influencers, you usually only have an opportunity to see what they want you to see. And usually it looks good.

How many times do you find yourself wanting to take on twenty or so of the different ideas you find yourself exposed to and expecting to complete them all in one week? We are not superhumans!

But, as normal humans, as flawed individuals, we start to compare: I wish I had more energy! I wish I was thinner. I wish my kids would obey. I wish my husband was more involved.

And typically we do all of this without realizing it.

Now, it's good to seek advice and ideas, but we all have to check ourselves and practice self-control. We need to learn how to recognize when to stop and when to continue seeking.

We need to have confidence in what we're doing. It's okay to make mistakes; everyone makes mistakes.

Julia Has a Gift

She excels at math. Julia got her master's degree in mathematics and taught high school at a local competitive charter school.

After giving birth to five kids, she decided to resign and homeschool exclusively. Each kid struggled with certain things. One child even had dyscalculia, also known as "number dyslexia." But Julia knew exactly what to do.

Her dedication even leaked into how she schooled language arts and the other subjects. Julia seemed so perfect at times. I mean, even her kids were well-behaved and proper. They were sweet and considerate.

But Julia never invited people over. Ever. And here is why:

She struggled. She struggled with keeping her home in order. Cooking, basic skills, and organizing were not her strong points. And it wasn't her kids that were the cause of the problem, either. It was an embarrassment, and she did everything she could to hide it.

Eventually, she realized that she had to do something about it. It was stressing her out. She had felt as though she had failed her children.

One day, she was chatting with her friends and it came up that their kids were struggling, too.

Bethany's child had a learning disability, and Bethany tried almost everything to correct it. It reared its head in all subjects, but especially math. She felt like she was failing him, frequently leading her to quit. She would erupt into tears whenever she talked about it.

But Bethany was also an organizer. She was gifted at keeping things tidy and in place. Her kids, too.

To make a long story short, Julia and Bethany worked together. These two ladies, with their different strengths, realized that they did, in fact, need each other. Both were flawed, but both had gifts. Neither of them was better than the other.

It takes a lot for someone to humble themselves and admit their faults and weaknesses, but when another friend, a family member, or even the community, comes alongside them to support them and even trade off skills, more blessings come.

We should never be ashamed of who we are and who we are meant to be. Many Christians believe that our confidence comes from God. He is the one who determines everything about us and every little skill we acquire. He wants us to be unique—and He wants us to lean on each other for help.

We should have confidence in that.

Think about how boring life would be if we were all the same. Why do we torture ourselves competing against the norm and then try to excel beyond the norm? We are constantly competing to be the best at everything, and it's just never possible.

It's the same for our kids. How many times have we compared our children to other children? To public school kids? To other homeschoolers? To grown-up kids? We are constantly wanting our kids to be the best, the nicest, and the smartest instead of who they are meant to be.

ADHD is a Gift

I have a dear friend who always says this. Whenever someone complains about their child's behavior, disorganization, scatter-brained moments, lost stuff, or what-have-you.

"They get so much done and with so much energy! Plus, hyper focus, girl! That is the ultimate superpower! Who cares if they've got multiple stitches or if they've broken many of your dishes? Yes, they need help in that area, and more attention, but they can do things that no one else can."

She's always thinking positively.

But I like that perspective—and to add to it, look who their parent is. It's you! And you have the special gift and responsibility of raising them. What a privilege! No one else could do it, and if you asked your child, they wouldn't want anyone but you to raise them, either. And that applies to most teenagers and middle schoolers. It does! Seriously!

Cookie Cutting

Every single person has the capability of adding something unique to this world. What would the world be without autism, ADHD, Down syndrome, dyslexia, cerebral palsy. They are not going to be considered "normal," ever. Why are we punishing them for that?

But what about when there is no disability? What if they just can't get math, or are they're poor at writing? What if they simply can't attain a certain score on the ACT or SAT? What if they appear to just enjoy working with their hands, or cleaning homes, or organizing things? Why do we think we have failed because they didn't become an engineer or pursue medical or law school?

It does come down to how we view this world. Are we viewing our kids through the lens of the Prussian Model, the public-school model, or are we using God's model? Are we relying on the world to dictate to us what our children are and who they should be? Are we punishing them for not living up to mainstream standards, or are we celebrating who they actually are?

Are we comparing our children to a cookie cutter?

"WE LIVE IN A DAY AND AGE WHERE CERTAIN PROFESSIONS ARE HONORED ABOVE OTHERS AND YET IF YOU DO WHAT YOU DO FOR THE GLORY OF GOD; IT HAS ETERNAL VALUE IN HIS SIGHT. HE CARES HOW YOU LABOR AND HE CARED ABOUT THE WAY YOU TREAT THOSE WITH WHOM AND WHOM YOU LABOR."

JAMES DAVIS

Chapter XX

PERMISSION

Now it's time to give yourself permission.

Permission to go against the grain.

Permission to work at the things you think are important.

Permission to not listen to those who put you down.

Permission to excel, to help your children excel in being who they are.

Give yourself permission to work, to work hard at discovering what meets your children's needs. Research finding them opportunities. Be persistent, and don't be discouraged.

Give yourself permission to stop when you are discouraged.

Give yourself permission to switch gears when things don't work. If a curriculum is causing you to fight or struggle too much, then stop using it. But also give yourself permission to find something new—even if it's into the middle of the year.

Give yourself permission to call a friend and lean on them for help. Admit that you need help. And in turn, give yourself permission to help others, knowing that you are capable, smart, and able.

Give yourself permission to recognize that your mindset and worldview may need to change. Give yourself permission to change.

Give yourself permission to be you. Don't think about what others are doing or what you need to do to prove yourself.

Give yourself permission to pray, to seek God in everything you do. Give yourself permission to listen to Him and allow Him to guide you.

It's time to move forward. Put the past behind you. Enjoy the little time you have and embrace—with confidence—what beautiful gifts you do have... homeschooling your kids.

Just give yourself permission. No matter what.

Permission

.

Chapter XXI

What Now?

Now you have work to do. You need time to reflect, write some goals, and get to work. But be inspired! You have a very special job, and no one in the world can do the job that you have been given.

Envision yourself and family twelve months from now. What kind of things do you want done? What kind of things do they want done? What do you want to be the center of your life? What does your life look like? Write it all down and enjoy.

If you want to connect with me and my family, I have a YouTube channel called Living With Eve. It shares with you tips, tricks, support, and ideas that will help you be the best you can be. I also share our journey as I raise my four kids, one with Down syndrome, in the homeschool world. I connect with my audience and we grow and learn, experiencing ups and downs together.

I would love to speak at conferences and retreats. My vision is to let every parent know that they can choose how their children are educated, that they are equipped, capable, and perfect for the job. It's our God-given right!

So on that note, let's keep in touch!

NOTES

_____

_____

_____

_____

_____

_____

_____

_____

_____

_____

_____

_____

_____

_____

_____

_____

_____

_____

_____

BIBLIOGRAPHY

1. Egyptian Eye. "Ancient Egyptian School." Egyptian Eye, Egyptian Eye, 2021, https://egyptianeye.net/ancient-egyptian-school/. Accessed 2 April 2021.

4. Focus on the Family. "The Purpose of the Family." Various Artist, June 29, 2017. http://www.focusonthefamily.com/parenting/the-purpose-of-the-family/ Accessed 7 April 2021.

5. Donald, Collins; Catheleen Jordan: Heather Coleman (2010) An Introduction to Family Social Work. Brooks/Cole, Cengage Learning pp. 28-29. ISBN 978-0-495-80872-5

6. Lander L. Howsare J, Byrne M. "The Impact of substance use disorders on families and children: From Theory To Practice. Soc Work Public Health 2013; 28:194-205

10. Quote by Katie Waalkes YouTube Channel "Life In The Mundane"

CITATIONS

Information about Rush: Rush, Benjamin (1970) [1948]. George Washington Corner (ed.). The autobiography of Benjamin Rush; his Travels through life together with his Commonplace book for 1789–1813. Westport, CT: Greenwood Press.

Document: https://explorepahistory.com/odocument.php?docId=1-4-218#:~:text=Benjamin%20Rush%2C%20%22Thoughts%20Upon%20the,the%20independence%20of%20our%20country.&text=The%20first%20remark%20that%20I,education%20in%20a%20foreign%20country.

https://www.stephenhicks.org/2009/12/29/fichte-on-education-as-socialization/

The Prussian Model: https://www.stgeorgeutah.com/news/archive/2012/03/14/our-prussian-model-of-public-schooling-controlling-the-masses/#.X83GnmhKjnY

European Universities from the Enlightenment to 1914 R. D. Anderson 2004 ISBN 978-0-19-820660-6 DOI:10.1093/acprof:oso/9780198206606.001.0001

Johann Fitch and Prussian Education Reform: https://feltd.wordpress.com/2010/09/16/the-prussian-german-educational-system/

Address to the German Nation:
https://en.wikisource.org/wiki/Addresses_to_the_German_Nation
(3) Horace Mann: Cubberley, Ellwood P. (1919). Public Education in the United States. p. 167.

Mondale, Sarah (2001). School: The Story of American Public Education. New York: Beacon.

(1)History of Standardized Tests - ProCon.org
(2) Gardner's Multiple Intelligences (tecweb.org)

Citations

ACKNOWLEDGMENTS

I first want to thank my best friend and love of my life, Eric, who continues to support me as I pursue my dreams. I also want to thank all of my kids who inspire me every day: Isaac, Ethan, Hannah, and Naomi. We do life together and it is wonderful.

I want to thank my Dad, Leslie, who has been bugging me to write a book forever and always encourages me with whatever I desire to do. A special thank you to my extended family for all the babysitting, listening to me ramble on about homeschooling, and encouraging me to take chances.

A special thank you to William & Lisa Walls for all of the tireless work they did to make this book possible and all of the extra advice and encouragement they offered to me along this process.

Thank you to all of my homeschool mama friends who have come alongside me on this journey—emotionally and spiritually: Crystal Crawford, Dina Fox, Valerie Castle, Rachel Guerrero, Joy Manroe, Katie Waalkes, Meghan Robinson, Ashley Weaver, Wendy Alcime, Yasmine Corona, Anna G., Rebecca Burton, Rian Smythe, Toni Studer, Sarah Rouse, Crystal Mitchell, Rachel Stewart, Annette Protani, Christy Freeman, Jamie Adams, Nina Baldwin, and many more.

Of course, this acknowledgment would not be complete without thanking the One I praise every day, who has given me breath, a mind, creativity, and much more that words cannot explain, My God and Savior, Yeshua. Plus, all of those people who He has brought around me to help me grow: Donna Britton, Carlene Cochran, and Rabbi Steve Weiler; I thank You for them.

ABOUT THE AUTHOR

Leilani was born and raised in Tampa, Florida. She attended public school and earned her degree at the University of Florida. Leilani began her teaching career as a middle school teacher at the age of 22. She taught everything from music and drama to Title I math and language arts.

After having her second son at 33, Leilani decided to resign and care for her two boys. As her family grew and her boys aged, homeschooling was her main teaching position.

Leilani has also fed into the local homeschool community by teaching classes at Class Source of Tampa, Inc. She has also been a member of F.I.S.H., a local homeschool co-op and the FPEA (Florida Parent Educators Association).

Since she still holds her teaching certificate for the State of Florida, another way that she supports the community is by evaluating and testing homeschoolers in the state of Florida so that they can meet the homeschool requirements.

After having her fourth child, a child with Down Syndrome, she has sought to bring awareness and support to struggling homeschool moms through her YouTube Channel, Living With Eve. This channel provides support, encouragement, and tips by sharing her journey from both a personal and professional perspective. Through this, she done several podcasts and online interviews.

To reach out to Leilani to have her speak at an event or interview, you can contact her at: Lei101978@hotmail.com.

81165861R00105